Conquering the STAGE

KIARA PIPINO | ALASKA REECE VANCE

Kendall Hunt
publishing company

Cover image was taken by the author.

Kendall Hunt
publishing company

www.kendallhunt.com
Send all inquiries to:
4050 Westmark Drive
Dubuque, IA 52004-1840

Published in the United States of America

Conquering the Stage

A Comprehensive Guide for the Actor

KIARA PIPINO and ALASKA REECE VANCE

This textbook is divided into fifteen weeks of training, which correspond to an academic semester. Each section translates into one week with two sessions. Sessions are meant to be experienced progressively. It would be best if actors shared their work with each other and had an instructor or outside eye to provide guidance and feedback. Each week includes an extra session in case aspiring actors want to pursue the topic in greater depth.

Contents

Week One Theatre Fundamentals   1

Session One: Vocabulary and Who's Who   3

Session Two: Stages and Stage positions   9

Go Deeper: The Father of Modern Acting   13

Week Two Step on Stage   17

Session One: Defeating Stage Fright   19

Session Two: Lean on Me   23

Go Deeper: Improv   27

Week Three Imagination   31

Session One: Look Around   33

Session Two: Recreate and Retell   35

Go Deeper: Imagine All the People   37

Week Four Memory   41

Session One: Awakening the Senses   43

Session Two: Can You Remember?   47

Go Deeper: It's Your Life!   51

Week Five Open Scenes   55

Session One: Do It!   57

Session Two: Switch It Up!   59

Go Deeper: Develop It!   61

Week Six Script and Characters   67

Session One: What's Happening?   69

Session Two: Who's Making It Happen?   73

Go Deeper: Research Is Fun!   75

Week Seven Script and Scenes   79
Session One: The Journey   81
Session Two: Touching the Scene   85
Go Deeper: Your Brand New World   87

Week Eight Personalizing Your World   91
Session One: Use Your Senses   93
Session Two: Create Your Journal   97
Go Deeper: Get on Your Feet   101

Week Nine Survive and Win   105
Session One: What Do I Want?   107
Session Two: How Do I Get It?   111
Go Deeper: Raising the Stakes   115

Week Ten Listening   119
Session One: You Are Not Alone   121
Session Two: Reacting to Your Partner   125
Go Deeper: Reacting to Your Space   127

Week Eleven Secrets and Surprises   131
Session One: Secrets   133
Session Two: Surprises   135
Go Deeper: Unexpected Gifts   137

Week Twelve Voice and Body   141
Session One: Voice   143
Session Two: Body   147
Go Deeper: Voice Meet Body   151

Week Thirteen The Director's View   155
Session One: The Director's Playground   157
Session Two: Your Playground   159
Go Deeper: Respect the Playwright!   161

Week Fourteen Monologues   163
Session One: What Is a Monologue?   165
Session Two: More than Words   169
Go Deeper: Pick the Right One!   173

Week Fifteen Auditioning   179
Session One: Etiquette   181
Session Two: Getting the Part   185
Go Deeper: A Professional Perspective   187

References   189
Index   191

Theatre Fundamentals

Introduction

Is Theatre an Art? or Is It a Craft? What Is Unique About Theatre?

Theatre is one of the most ancient forms of expression.

This is not the place for a thorough investigation of theatre history, so we won't indulge in too much historical data. However, it is important for aspiring young actors to be aware that the first known independent actor was Thespis, who performed in Athens, Greece, in the 4th Century B.C.

Thespis' legacy lives on today and he is remembered all over the world; why, even his own name now stands for "actor"! If you call yourself a thespian, you are likely calling yourself an actor.

Interestingly, in ancient Greece, the term for "actor" was "hypokrites", which meant "someone pretending to be someone else". As you might have guessed, our word "hypocrite" is rooted in that ancient Greek word, although its meaning has acquired a negative connotation. If someone calls you a big hypocrite today, you certainly won't be flattered.

But, returning to our original questions, let's briefly analyze Theatre as a form of human expression.

Can We Call Theatre an Art Form?

If you look at the definition of art, you will discover that in order for something to be considered a "work of art", there has to be a creative process involving imagination and interpretation. Every work of art, whether it's a painting, a drawing, a sculpture, etc., is uniquely connected to someone's creativity and personal elaboration of something: an idea, a visual, a sound. And here we have the tricky part: is our beloved chocolate cake a work of art? After all, it is our own personal interpretation of a recipe, and we sure use imagination in order to give it a kick and to make it pretty.

Well, as much as that might be true, a work of art has to be something that is created with the intention of making an artistic statement. Art has no "practical" function. We would all agree that there isn't much of an artistic statement or intention in our chocolate cake: it's made to feed stomachs rather than minds. Our chocolate cake has a (wonderful) practical function.

Theatre indeed qualifies as a form of art, as it is the result of someone – an actor, a playwright, a performer, or a director – who intentionally elaborates a concept that translates into storytelling through the mouths of fictional characters.

More importantly, Theatre is **unique** among the other forms of art because it changes every time. By that, we mean that every performance is different, even if the script stays the same. Theatre is "live" and experiences all the advantages and disadvantages of that situation. Think about it: Shakespeare wrote *Hamlet* around 1602, but it's still one of the most produced plays of all time. Why? Because every production is a new interpretation of that script and because every night, the actors will react somewhat differently as a result of many factors, including their personal physical and psychological conditions, the audience response, the technical elements, and so on and so forth.

Can anyone do Theatre? Yes, as much as anyone can paint or sculpt. Having something to say and wanting to express it artistically through theatre is surely enough to inspire anyone to pursue their passion. Remember though: talent alone doesn't suffice; otherwise, there would be plenty of Michelangelos and Van Goghs. Talent can show you the way and help you find your motives, but, for the fulfillment of your artistic endeavors, training is just as important. Training provides you with tools and knowledge to support your ideas and better develop them. Potentially, you could be the greatest actor of your generation, but if your voice doesn't carry the lines and convey your passion, no one will hear you. If you do not exercise your memory and your imagination, you will not be able to make sense of the character; you won't make strong enough choices and you won't remember your lines.

So finally, yes, Theatre is a form of art. It is a unique form of art because of its "live" nature. But Theatre is also a craft, as skills are developed and perfected through training and commitment.

What Do You Need to Do Theatre?

As you look around nowadays, you find such an incredible variety of theatrical experiences that it might be confusing to really understand what is at the heart of it all: what is really necessary in order to have theatre.

It all goes back to Thespis: an actor, telling a story, to the audience.

Sure, the director is important. Of course, the scenery helps tell the story. But the director needs someone on stage to tell the story, and a scenery with no actors becomes an empty frame or a beautiful picture. Therefore, aspiring actors: rejoice! Without you, there would be no theatre. But remember, you need to have a story to tell and someone to tell it to.

Session One

Vocabulary and Who's Who

Vocabulary

In this session, we'll provide you some important terms that you should familiarize yourself with in order to better communicate with other theatre artists.

The *script* is the text of the play you are working on. It is not a screenplay: that is the text of a movie. Scripts are usually divided into acts and scenes. In a production, you might often hear talk of the *French Scene Breakdown*.

A *French Scene* defines a section of the play that begins with a character's entrance and finishes with that same character's exit. French Scenes are often tied to the character that accomplishes the most during his/her presence on stage. There are typically many French Scenes in a play, they are usually interconnected and of course they are not created by the same character throughout the whole play. The French Scene Breakdown is important because it gives the creative team an understanding of how much time each character is or isn't on stage, which leads to, for example, costume change choices. Sometimes, directors arrange their rehearsal schedule around the French Scene Breakdown, rather than following the script's Act and Scene divisions; therefore, it's important for the actors to understand what it means.

Another way of dividing the script is by using *beats*.

A *beat* defines a unity in action. For example: characters A and B are fighting. The corresponding beat might start with the beginning of the fight and end with its resolution.

Careful! When you read a script, sometimes you will find the word "beat" written in parenthesis and italics in between the dialogue. In that case, it is part of the *stage directions* and it only means a moment of silence.

The *stage directions* are not part of the storytelling; they are just a way to mark all the things that the actors – not the characters – are doing on stage as they are portraying their characters. They can be part of the script, but not part of the show. Sometimes, stage directions are written by the playwright. Tennessee Williams is famous for writing very articulate and specific stage directions, as he wanted the whole creative team to get a full understanding of the environment of the play. Other times, and more often in contemporary playwriting, stage directions are written by the stage manager or by the director of a past production, and are meant to show what decisions were made in that specific production – usually the original one.

To be "*off book*" means to have the lines fully memorized for the character you are playing. Directors make the off book date (the day the actors must be "off book") very clear in their rehearsal schedules. Often in the professional world, actors are required to be "off book" on the first day of rehearsals.

To rehearse *script in hand*, means that the actors are allowed to carry the script on stage and look at it while they are working. Clearly, the option to hold the script can be a blessing, because you can rely on it, but at the same time, it can also be a curse, as it can impede your movement. When you are rehearsing "script in hand", it's important to familiarize yourself with your lines so that you can have as much freedom of movement and engagement as possible.

To *call line* is when an actor, while performing in a rehearsal, asks the stage manager or the assistant stage manager for a line he or she doesn't remember. The line will then be fed to them and they can continue working without going back to their script.

A *cue* is something: a word, a gesture, a light change, a scenic change, an entrance, etc. that triggers an action or a change. When you hear the director asking you to "*pick up your cue*", it means that your reaction to something needs to happen sooner in order not to interrupt the flow of the story telling.

(photo credit: sirtravelalot/shutterstock.com)

For example, characters Alice and Bertram are talking about the imminent arrival of Chuck.

Alice:	Chuck is going to be here any minute now and he's going to be wondering what to do for dinner.
Bertram:	I forgot to get groceries!
Alice:	And there's nothing in the fridge!
	(Chuck enters from UL)
Chuck:	Hey guys! What's for dinner? I'm starving!

The actor playing Chuck needs to enter as soon as he hears "fridge!" That is his cue. *(Chuck Enters from Upstage Left)* is an example of a stage direction, which implies that in a past staging of this scene, the actor playing Chuck was told to enter from upstage left. As you can very well imagine, nothing suggests that in a different production of this scene, the actor playing that role could not enter from say, Right Center, instead. In other words, most of the times stage directions are suggestions; they provide a solution to a problem or simply are one option to justify the dialogue. Actors and directors are usually free to change the staging and alter the stage directions as long as they do not betray the text.

Attention! The dialogue (i.e. the words that characters say to one another) cannot be changed, at least for those plays that are protected by copyright. Actors cannot choose to paraphrase a line, because they get idea of what their character is saying, but they don't feel like memorizing the exact words.

Cues are also important for the technical elements of the production.

For example:

Alice:	I wonder when Chuck is going to be here.
Bertram:	He said would come at eight.
	(The doorbell rings)
Alice:	Aha! Here he is!

The sound cue of a doorbell needs to happen when Bertram says "at eight". Regardless of whether the sound cue is recorded or live, whoever operates it will wait for Bertram to say "at eight". If Bertram says "soon" instead of "at eight", the result could be a "dead" moment, because whoever is operating the doorbell is waiting to hear "at eight" and might take a second to recognize the mistake and operate the sound cue. In the meantime, Alice would have a moment of panic, which would interfere with her acting. Sure, no one is going to die because of the blunder, but still: learn your lines!

A fun fact about cues: Theatre folk tend to be superstitious and there are peculiar superstitions related to theatre. One of them is that you should not whistle on stage (unless it's required by the script). Why? Because in the past the backstage crew communicated in a code of whistles to operate scenery and lights. If an actor absentmindedly whistled a tune, it could potentially be dangerous, because it could very well be a cue for something to happen!

There are many terms that you will learn as you continue in your acting journey. A lot of them relate to your approach to the character and the script and will inform your acting vocabulary. We will focus on many of those terms in Week Six: Scripts and Characters.

Group Exercise: Small Group Script Work

Note for the group leader/instructor: For this exercise, you will need to provide a copy of the same script for each small group.

Step 1 – Divide
Divide into small groups and look over your script together. Begin breaking your script into French Scenes (you might stop when you have identified three French Scenes). Now divide your first French Scene into "beats". Also, note any examples of stage directions in your first French Scene.

Step 2 – Compare
Come together with the whole group. Compare your small group's decisions and discoveries with those of the other small groups.

Who's Who in Theatre

Actors! It's important that you know, and respect, all the people collaborating with you in the artistic journey that will lead to opening night. Here is a breakdown of some of the personnel who may be involved in your next theatre production.

The playwright is the author of the play. The playwright created the story and "owns" it. It's your job to bring it to life while respecting the playwright's intentions. If you're working on a contemporary script, chances are that the playwright is alive and well and that his or her work is protected by copyright.

Copyright covers all the works that have been written in the last seventy years.

Violations to copyright are persecuted by the law.

The script usually includes copyright information: make sure you read it all!

Nowadays, playwrights tend to work more closely with the rest of the artistic team and often they actively participate in rehearsals. An example of this participation lies in the many new play festivals, such as the Humana Festival of New American Plays in Louisville KY, that happen all around the world.

The producer is the one who "makes it happen" economically. He or she supervises and operates the economic part of the project, by hiring everyone involved, finding a space to rehearse, defining marketing strategies, and so on. The producer takes the economic pressure off the artistic team and sometimes he/she also participates in the artistic decisions. For example, on Broadway, it's not unusual for producers to cast the show before even identifying a director. The producer is usually the one taking the economic risks or responsibility in the production; he/she finds and invests the money to fund the production and if it fails, he/she is the one who lost it all.

The director has the job of interpreting the script and recreating a consistent world for the actors to play with. He or she develops a concept, or a vision, that needs to be communicated to everyone involved in the production so that everyone can contribute to it according to their function, skills, and talents. The director is also the first audience member; he/she gets to see the show "in the making" and has to make sure that the storytelling is clear from an acting, as well as from a technical, standpoint. He/she needs to make sure that the blocking is consistent, that all the actors are clearly seen on stage and that all the other elements (lights, sound, scenery, props, etc.) occur consistently in the story telling. The director also usually casts the show: he/she holds auditions and decides which actor will play each role. The director's job ends on opening night.

The dramaturg brings his or her specific knowledge about some aspects of the production. His/her job is mostly related to researching and providing cultural support to the director and the actors. For example, Shakespearian productions often take advantage of a dramaturg to better understand the language and the historical references. Or if the play deals with, say, a specific disease, a physician might be asked to be the dramaturg to share his or her experience on the matter. Sometimes, theatre companies will employ a resident dramaturg.

The scenic designer is in charge of visually recreating the world of the play. His or her design will be influenced by a collaboration with the director and the other theatre artists involved in the production as well as by the nature of the space in which the production will take place. The scenic designer will produce models of the design and technical drawings, which will be given to the **technical director** who will physically execute them and build the set. Sometimes the scenic designer is also in charge of the props, although usually this job falls to the **properties master.** Props are the objects that the actors carry on or off stage or handle. (For example, a candle is a prop; a coffee table is not.)

The costume designer is responsible for everything the actors are wearing on stage. The costume designer's job is to investigate the character and create his or her wardrobe. If the play is set in a specific historical time, it's the job of the costume designer to do research so that costumes will be consistent with that period. The costume designer will also make sure that the costumes will respond to both the needs of the play and of the actors. For example, if a character needs to be in a suit in Act One, Scene One and then in totally different attire in Act One, Scene Two, and the actor playing that role has very little time to change off stage, the costumer will design the suit in such a way as to allow for a "quick change". The costumer will create sketches and renderings of the costumes for the director to see and will provide the **costume shop manager** with the technical drawings. The costume shop manager, the stitchers, the drapers, and all the costume shop personnel will then acquire or build the costumes.

The lighting designer provides focus to the play and creates the mood of each moment/scene via the lights. His or her job starts with researching the world of the play, its locations, the times of day for every scene and the emotional scenarios of specific moments. He/she must work collaboratively with all the other designers, since lights can significantly change the perception of a scene and impact both the costumes and the scenery. If the production involves projections, either the lighting designer or the scenic designer will be in charge of them. The lighting designer will create a light plot, which will be handed to the **master electrician** who will then proceed with hanging and focusing the lights.

The sound designer, like all the other designers involved in the production, is in charge of contributing in creating the world of the play by creating the required sounds. Those sounds can be executed live or can be recorded and then played on cue. The sound designer is also responsible for any microphones that are utilized. The sound designer might be in charge of creating original tracks. He or she might put together a soundtrack to "underscore" the scenes, to prepare the audience for the play before the show begins, or to be played during intermission.

The stage manager is the director's right hand. He or she is the interface between the director and the actors when it comes to practicalities: providing the rehearsal schedules, communicating conflicts, handling call times, etc. He/she makes sure that everything needed for an efficient rehearsal is readily accessible. He/she serves as the liaison between the director and the other theatre artists. During rehearsals, the stage manager writes the blocking on his/her script so that a written record of everything is available if needed. The stage manager will also mark on the script all the technical cues of the show. The stage manager's script is part of his/her promptbook, which also includes the contact information of everyone involved in the production, technical information about the set, props, costumes, etc., schedules, and any other paperwork that is needed to facilitate a smoothly run production. Once the show opens, the stage manager's job is to "call the show", that is, run the show by calling all the cues. He/she does this by being on headset with the light board operator, the soundboard operator and the **assistant stage manager** backstage.

This breakdown gives you an idea of the personnel that are most commonly part of a theatrical production. There are of course many other theatrical occupations that tackle even more specific aspects of the show. For example, in a musical, the **choreographer** envisions the dancing, while the **music director** is in charge of teaching actors the score. If dialects are used, quite likely a vocal coach will be involved and if there is a fight in the show, there will be a **fight choreographer.**

Finally, any discussion of theatre occupations would be incomplete without mentioning all the hard-working people who are busy backstage during the show: the **crew.** They ensure that scene changes actually happen smoothly and on time, help the actors get in and out of their costumes, clean the costumes after every show, reset everything at the end of the show so that it will be ready for the next performance, and much more; all in the quest for a seamless production!

Group Exercise: Job Descriptions

Sit in a circle with your group. Going around the circle, have each group member take a turn naming one theatre duty discussed above. Have the group discuss and determine which theatrical job includes that particular duty.

Terms to Remember:

Script	Producer	Master Electrician
French Scene	Director	Sound Designer
Beat	Dramaturg	Stage Manager
Stage Directions	Scenic Designer	Assistant Stage Manager
Off Book	Technical Director	Choreographer
Script in Hand	Properties Master	Music Director
Call Line	Costume Designer	Fight Choreographer
Cue	Costume Shop Manager	Crew
Playwright	Lighting Designer	

Stages and Stage Positions

Theatre Spaces and How They Inform and Influence the Acting

There are many spaces where Theatre can be experienced. Below are the most common.

The Proscenium Stage

The most well-known performance space is without a doubt the proscenium theatre. In this space, the audience sits in front of the stage, which is usually elevated from the ground. The actors face the audience, entering and exiting from the right or left wings or from the back of the stage. The proscenium theatre is the space that perhaps best creates the illusion of a fictional reality, as there is a clear separation between the world of the play and the spectators. We call this separation "the fourth wall". This type of space usually facilitates a spectacular array of scenic and light possibilities, with scenes that can transition seamlessly (the "magic of theatre"), thanks to the backstage area and to the space above the stage (the fly loft).

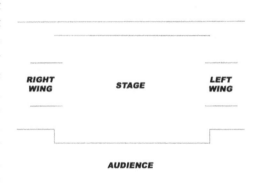

The proscenium theater was the most common type of theatrical space from the 18th Century until well into the 20th Century. Most colleges and universities offer a proscenium theatre as their main stage option, and most Broadway theaters are proscenium theatres. The proscenium stage is usually "framed" by an arch, the proscenium arch, which functions like the frame of a picture. Therefore, actors need to make sure their movement on stage – that is, their **blocking** – allows everyone to be seen and provides a balanced, harmonious picture.

Thrust

The thrust configuration has the stage projecting itself into the house, with the audience facing its three sides. It's basically a wider catwalk, which allows the actors to be closer to the audience. Entrances and exits usually happen from upstage, and scene changes tend to be minimal as they have to occur in sight of the audience, masked only by fading lights. This means the audience sees some technical aspects of the production in addition to the story telling.

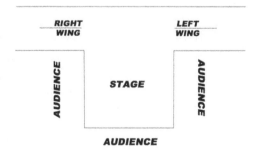

The thrust has become increasingly popular due to the greater popularity of more intimate shows with smaller casts and smaller budgets. The thrust is also a frequent solution in those situations where the theatrical space is the result of the renovation of a building, which originally served a non-theatrical purpose.

When acting on a thrust, actors need to adjust their blocking to allow the audience to have a clear view and understanding of the dynamics of the scene. Since the audience is on three sides of the stage, quite likely the actors will be giving their backs to the spectators at some point. Still, they can make sure that the audience sees at least one of the actors' faces for most of the performance. When directing in a thrust, directors tend to prefer using diagonals in their blocking patterns, to help with visibility and sightlines for the audience.

Arena

The arena space is the most difficult theatrical space when it comes to acting and directing, as the audience is all around the stage. This makes it impossible for the actors not to be giving their backs to the audience at any point during the performance. A way to minimize this disadvantage is to keep the blocking very dynamic (just make sure it's not so dynamic that it creates a hectic scene!). In the arena stage, there is usually less opportunity for the "magic of theatre" to happen; technical equipment is most of the time very visible and set pieces coming on and off stage have to come from the house, with the audience seeing all. Arena Theaters are sometimes call "theatre in the round".

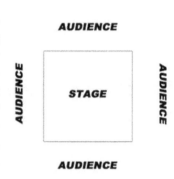

The Black Box

As the term suggests, the Black Box is a room, usually rectangular in shape, that has the walls and floor painted black. It's a multifunctional theatrical space, because it can accommodate several configurations of the stage and the audience area. The ceiling of the room is generally able to offer multiple rigging solutions for lights and sound, making the entire use of the space extremely flexible. Black Boxes can be configured as proscenium, thrust or arena theaters. This type space is very popular as a studio theatre or a second stage. Many universities and large theatres companies have Black Box theaters as rehearsal spaces or performance spaces for more intimate shows. It is rare for a Black Box to seat two hundred people; more likely it would accommodate around one hundred. As a result, this space tends to be very intimate with the actors performing closer to the audience. This means that the acting has to be more detailed, and the actors have to be comfortable with the situation.

Open Air Theatre and Other Spaces

Theatre companies and actors also perform in spaces that do not fall into any of the above categories. Many summer festivals or Off Broadway venues locate themselves in "**found spaces**", like parks, gardens, monuments, various outdoor locations, abandoned warehouses, repurposed buildings, and so on. In this case, the acting becomes "site-specific".

For example, the British theatre company Punchdrunk has been presenting their show *Sleep No More* in the McKittrick Hotel in New York City since 2011. The show is an adaptation of Shakespeare's *Macbeth*. As the audience walks in, everyone is handed a white mask, which they have to wear for the entirety of their stay in the "hotel". The space is a three-story building, which was once a hotel and has been redesigned for the needs of the show. The actors/performers aren't wearing masks and move freely

(photo credit: © Kiara Pipino)

in the building, following the script. The audience can decide which characters to follow and for how long. Each room is fully scenographed, and since the audience can interact with the space, the props and scenery are as real as they can be.

Other times, often in the summer, shows are presented in open air spaces: think of all the "Shakespeare in the Park" festivals around the world. Even if those situations are well serviced from a technical standpoint, acting outside is rather different than acting indoors. Actors might have to adjust to projecting louder than usual or wearing mics and keeping their focus (and the audiences focus) despite distractions such as weather, traffic, and so on.

Group Discussion: Theatre Spaces

In which types of theatre spaces have you watched plays or performances? Which type did you enjoy most as an audience member? Least? Which type of theatre space seems most challenging for actors or designers? Why? As an actor, which type of theatre space do you think you would enjoy most? Why?

Positions on Stage/Blocking

All the movements that actors do on stage are called *blocking*. It's important for the actors to know the names of the different stage positions because that will facilitate communication between them and everyone else involved in the production: the director, the stage manager, the designers, the crew, and so on. Positions on stage do not vary according to the type of stage (with the exception of the arena stage, in which case an agreement will have to be made among everyone involved in the production). The audience sits in what is normally referred as **the house**. Let's look at the template of the proscenium theatre for an example.

The stage faces the house and the actors face the audience. We call *downstage* the area of the stage that is closer to the audience. *Upstage* would be the area that is further away from the house and closer to the back of the theater. Left and right are determined by the position of the actors, if the actors are facing the audience. If actor A is on stage facing the audience, *stage right* would be the area on the actor's right, which would correspond to the area on the left of the audience. Similarly, *stage left* would be the area on the actor's left side – the audience's right side. So *stage right* corresponds to *house left* and *stage left* corresponds to *house right*. *Center stage* refers to the area at the center of the stage. The stage is also subdivided into smaller areas: *upstage right, upstage center, upstage left, center right, center stage, center left, downstage right, downstage center,* and *downstage left*. If the director asks the actor to "cross downstage left from upstage center", you will see the actor walking towards the audience on his or her left.

Group Exercise: Blocking Memorization Game

Step 1 – Divide
Divide your group into two teams.

Step 2 – Team A's Blocking
The group leader/instructor gives Team A a list of three stage directions (e.g., the leader might say, "enter the stage right, cross to center left and pause, then cross upstage left"). Together the team must execute the directions.

Step 3 – Team B's Blocking
The group leader gives Team B a different list of three stage directions. Together the team must execute those directions.

Step 4 – More for A
The leader gives another stage direction to Team A. Team A must add the stage direction to their list and complete all four of their stage directions by memory.

Step 5 – More for B
The leader gives another stage direction to team B. Team B must add the stage direction to their list and complete all four of their stage directions by memory.

Step 6 – Escalate
Continue adding another stage direction to the lists. When one of the teams makes a mistake on their blocking, that team is "out".

Step 7 – Round Two and Beyond
Divide the winning team into two new teams and repeat play from step two. Continue to divide the winning teams from each round until you are down to only two actors. The two actors can then play for the title of "Blocking Champion"!

Terms to Remember:

Proscenium	Black Box	Upstage
Blocking	Open Air Theatre	Downstage
Thrust	Found Spaces	Stage Left
Arena	House	Stage Right

The Father of Modern Acting

Constantin Stanislavski

Constantin Stanislavski (Moscow, Russia 1863–1938) is one of the most influential stage actors and directors of all time. He dedicated his life to developing his most famous acting technique, known as the Stanislavski Technique or Method Acting.

Stanislavski came from a wealthy family who loved the arts, and theatre in particular. He started his acting career very young and eventually moved to Russia's capital city, Moscow, where he founded a theatre company called "The Society of Art and Literature". He acted in and directed several productions for The Society. Later he moved to the newborn Moscow Art Theatre, where he spent the rest of his career. The Moscow Art Theatre produced new, exciting works, including all of Anton Chekov's plays. Stanislavski either directed or acted in most of them.

The artistic partnership between Chekhov and Stanislavski led to the conception and pursuit of a new style of acting, which was less presentational and rhetorical and more true to life. Stanislavski wanted the actors to portray characters that were believable and authentic, like real people, and Chekhov's plays offered such characters.

The Method is a technique that helps actors connect with their emotions, develop a creative imagination and eventually leads them to a truthful performance on stage. Elements of The Method include "the magic if". Stanislavski wanted the actors to ask themselves: "What would I do if I were in that situation?", so that they could put themselves into the character's shoes. If they did that, they would inevitably personalize and believe in what they did and said on stage. Sensory Memory is another key element in The Method. Sensory Memory is a subconscious database of emotions, feelings, and experiences that everyone has and yet very few access or utilize. Everything we experience in life becomes part of our emotional database through our senses and can be relived through our senses. In order to be truthful on stage, The Method teaches that actors need to relive – not just recall – those experiences in order to evoke the emotion the character is supposed to be living in.

Stanislavski created a whole new vocabulary and array of exercises to specifically help actors find their motives (Objectives) and strategies (Actions). Finally, Stanislavski was famous for "people watching". He would spend hours observing people so that he could learn gestures, habits and behaviors to eventually utilize in performance. He strongly believed that all actors should do the same.

Stanislavski's legacy has influenced, and still influences, actors' training all over the world. His technique is considered the foundation of acting and he is considered the father of modern acting. Among some of his most famous followers are Stella Adler, Uta Hagen, and Lee Strasberg, who founded the Actors' Studio in NYC, importing his work to the United States.

Group Exercise: People Watching

(Note: This exercise should only be done if in an appropriate situation, like a college campus. For groups/classes in which this exercise would not be suitable, you can use the discussion questions to discussion observations you've made about human behavior in the past.)

Step 1 – Watch
Spread out and find a location where you can watch people in action. Spend at least ten minutes studying people. Try to notice specific behaviors and individual qualities and quirks. Assume that everything has meaning. Try to imagine what is behind every movement, however miniscule.

Step 2 – Discuss
Return to the group and discuss your findings and observations. What was the most interesting habit or quirk that you observed? What did you notice while "people watching" that you normally miss in everyday life? What did it feel like to be still and observe? Was it difficult to stay focused on observation? Do you enjoy "people watching"? Why or why not? Why do you think that Stanislavsky thought observing others would be helpful to actors? As an aspiring actor, do you think you would benefit from more "people watching"?

Worksheet

Week One – Theatre Fundamentals

Recall three performances you have participated in or observed. Answer the questions related to each production.

Production #1 _____

What type of theatre space was utilized? _____

How did the theatre space affect the production? _____

_____

What did you find most memorable about the performance and why? _____

_____

Which theatre professional do you think had the most impact on that particular aspect of the performance and why? _____

_____

_____

Production #2 _____

What type of theatre space was utilized? _____

How did the theatre space affect the production? _____

_____

What did you find most memorable about the performance and why? _____

_____

Which theatre professional do you think had the most impact on that particular aspect of the performance and why? _____

_____

_____

Production #3 _____

What type of theatre space was utilized? _____

How did the theatre space affect the production? _____

_____

What did you find most memorable about the performance and why? _____

_____

Which theatre professional do you think had the most impact on that particular aspect of the performance and why? _____

_____

_____

Week Two

Step on Stage

Introduction

Now that we've gone over some theatre basics, it's time to leave your seat and put your feet on the stage. Because stepping on stage can be intimidating for most, let's spend some time exploring strategies to defeat stage fright and thrive in front of any audience.

Defeating Stage Fright

Stage fright presents itself in many forms: butterflies in the stomach, inability to project, dry mouth, trembling hands . . . you name it. Most people have experienced it in one form or another and nobody likes it, but by naming it, examining it, and learning some coping strategies, you don't have to be paralyzed by it. Nelson Mandela said "The brave man is not he who does not feel afraid, but he who conquers that fear". Let's take a step towards conquering our fears.

Group Exercise: Checking In

Step 1 – "Check-In"
Stand in a circle on the stage with your group. The first actor should say his or her name accompanied by a motion that expresses how he or she is feeling at that very moment. The rest of the group should repeat the name and the motion back to the first actor. The activity should continue around the circle until everyone has performed his or her name with a motion. Note: When performing your motion, try not to use motions that are too "literal" or that are universal gestures. For example, if you are feeling tired, instead of laying your head on your folded hands, try letting your current state-of-being express itself through your muscles, limbs, face, etc. Use your imagination and think outside of the box!

Step 2 – "Check-In" with Focus on Performance
Discuss getting up on stage in front of an audience. Close your eyes and picture what that would feel like. Repeat the "Check-In" part of the exercise from above, using motions that express how the idea of performing makes you feel.

Step 3 – Discuss
Who is nervous? Who is excited? Who is apprehensive? Why do you believe the thought of performing evokes that particular response in you?

Congratulations! You just stood onstage and delivered a line (your name) accompanied by expressive physical action in front of an audience. You took the first step in overcoming fear of performance: time onstage.

Now we're going to share with you a secret that could change your theatrical life. Are you ready? Hold on to your hat because it's a good one. **Nerves are your allies.** Did you hear that? You might think we're pulling your leg, but we're raising our right hands while saying it a second time. Nerves are your allies! Say it. "Nerves are my allies." It feels good to say that, doesn't it? And the best thing about it is it's true.

Even experienced actors get nervous before performing in front of an audience; the trick is *using* that feeling rather than fighting against it. First, let's change the way we think about this anxiety, or stage fright, or nervousness. Let's instead call it nervous energy. Although it might make your stomach a little queasy, this nervous energy is going to give you power onstage. Your character is going to use this nervous energy to achieve goals in the scene. This nervous energy is going to bring more life, excitement, and importance to the scene. This nervous energy is going to bring clarity and focus as you pursue your goals and interact with the others onstage. All this is possible if you choose to embrace your nervous energy and use it for good. Actors who fight against their nerves can be overcome by them, causing a distracted, fumbling, and/or weak performance. If you think you can defeat your stage fright by willing it away, think again. In fact, stage fright can only be "defeated" by turning it from foe to friend.

(photo credit: Mazan Xeniya/Shutterstock.com)

Group Exercise: Colorful Nerves and Dreams

Step 1 – Greet
Find a partner and a space in the room to sit together. Spend some time getting to know each other.

Step 2 – Share
"Partner A" shares with "Partner B" a personal dream or goal that they have not shared with many people and why this dream or goal is important to them. "Partner B" then shares with "Partner A".

Step 3 – Imagine
Separate. Find your own space in the room. Spend a few minutes thinking about your partner and the dream they just shared with you. Imagine yourself as your partner. What is your life like? What circumstances have molded you into the person you are today? Have you been encouraged or discouraged in perusing your dream? Remember, when considering the above questions, you are imagining yourself as your partner. Use your imagination to fill in the information that you are not privy to.

Step 4 – Visualize
You are about to "perform" the role of your partner in front of the group. You might be feeling a little nervous (or very nervous). Remind yourself that nerves are your allies. Find a spot where you can lie down on your back. The instructor should then lead the group through the following visualization:

> Take a deep breath. Imagine that you're allowing the breath to flow deep into your stomach, filling it up and expanding your stomach and then chest cavity. Continue to breathe deeply as you picture yourself standing in front of the group. Allow yourself to feel nervous energy. Try to imagine the nerves fluttering inside you. In your minds' eye, give form and color to the nerves. What do they look like and where are they located? Use your imagination and creativity. Continue to breathe deep as you picture the nerves. Enjoy the sensations they give. Picture each nerve as an individual, awesome power source, ready for you to grab, and use as needed. With your next deep breath in, grab one of those nerves. Discharge the nerve with a powerful exhale. Repeat. With each breath in, grab some of those wonderful nerves inside and exhale them with power.

Step 5 – Perform

Return to the group. Take turns stepping onstage and playing the "role" of your partner. Become your partner as you introduce "yourself" to the group, and share "your" dream or goal. Remember to honor the person you are playing by being respectful of the goal or dream they shared. They trusted you with something precious, don't mock or make light of the information. As you are "performing" you may feel those nerves attempting to overcome you. If you feel them, visualize grabbing them and using them to add depth and importance to your words.

Step 6 – Discuss

The group should come together and discuss the components of the exercise. Was it difficult to imagine yourself as your partner? Why or why not? How did it feel to visualize nerves as physical entities? What did your "nerves" look like? Were you able to commit to the visualization? Did the visualization help you see your nerves in a more positive light? Did the visualization help you to use your nerves to your advantage? How did it feel to watch someone perform as you onstage and hear them share your personal dream? Did you feel closer to your partner after portraying him/her onstage?

We have discussed befriending our nervous energy and using it to our advantage. If you remember that nerves are your allies, you will recurrently reap the benefits of this mindset through all your work onstage. Are you still concerned that stage fright is going to overpower you? Not to worry. You have an ace up your sleeve, and that ace is your scene partner. When you are fully engaged with your scene partner, listening to them and trusting them, debilitating stage fright will become a thing of the past. If you are listening to your scene partner (really listening) and communicating (really communicating) with them, you'll have a lot less time to focus on your fear. Whenever you start to feel afraid, turn your attention to your partner and listen closely. We will continue our discussion on working with others in the next session and we'll delve deep into the skill of listening later in the book.

Lean on Me

In the previous session we discussed how we can use our nervous energy to produce powerful, exciting characters. If we learn to harness them, our nerves can become our allies onstage, keeping us focused and engaged. We have other allies onstage that are even more potent than our nerves. Can you guess who they are? If you guessed your scene partners, you are absolutely correct.

In theatre, a **company** is a group of actors, technicians and theatre artists who work together on a production or series of productions. As we work through this book, let's agree that our classmates are our company. A company is a lot like a team. Everyone has to work together to make the show a success. If a quarterback is doing a fantastic job but the rest of the team comes to the field to play baseball, will the team win the super bowl? A hockey team could have the best goalie alive, but if the team can't skate, they're not going to win the championship. If a basketball team is populated by players who don't believe in passing, will the team succeed? Just like in sports, actors must work together, trust each other, and *play the same game* if they want the show to be a success.

Group Exercise: Qualities of a Teammate

Step 1 – List
Take a few minutes as a group to make a list of qualities that you believe would make a good teammate on a sports team. Decide on the top five qualities a good teammate should possess.

Step 2 – Discuss
Discuss the qualities on your list and decide which would also make a good theatre company member. Decide on the top five qualities a good theatre company member should possess. Is the top five list the same? If not, how does it differ and why?

Actors need their "teammates" just as much as any athlete. Actors put themselves in vulnerable situations often as they use their imaginations to experience the difficult and varied needs and desires of their characters, often resulting in deep emotional experiences. It's profoundly important that company members trust each other onstage, regardless of their relationship offstage. The most enjoyable, successful companies have members who trust each other offstage as well. Determine now to cultivate the qualities in yourself that will make you a great scene partner and company member.

Group Discussion: Theatre Games

Have you ever noticed that actors play a lot of seemingly silly games? These "theatre games" are designed to build a sense of community, spark creativity and help actors listen to, and trust each other. What is your experience with "theatre games" or "warm-up games"? Do you have a favorite? Share your favorite games with your group discuss how each particular game might help an actor. Choose one or more of these games to play now.

Earlier we mentioned that actors in a company, just like players on a field, must be "playing the same game". Perhaps you were puzzled by that statement. Acting is acting right? Well, there are many different styles of theatre, different worlds created, and different times and places represented onstage. When acting in a company all actors must be living in the same "world" for the story to be believable. Even campy comedy or children's theatre seeks to whisk the audience into the world of the play. A world that is consistent and unified will help to facilitate the audience's **suspension of disbelief** or willingness to accept the unbelievable.

Exercise: Planet Customs

Step 1 – Planet Assignments
Divide the group into four smaller units. The leader should assign each group a planet from the list below and share with them the four customs or values that are important to their planet. The groups should name their planets and decide on a few more customs or values for their planet to uphold.

Planet A
In this world, people talk in very loud voices. It is considered rude to be quiet.
In this world, people are very animated.
In this world, people desire a large amount of personal space, even while conversing.
In this world, frowning is considered an insult.

Planet B
In this world, people talk in very quiet voices. It is considered rude to be loud.
In this world, it is very important to compliment everyone constantly.
In this world, jumping is the hottest new trend.
In this world, people always use their hands when they converse.

Planet C
In this world, showing the palms of your hands is extremely rude.
In this world, asking personal questions is rude, but honesty is important.
In this world, people get very close to each other when the converse.
In this world, silliness is highly valued.

Planet D
In this world, smiling is considered an insult.
In this world, looking at people directly is considered rude.
In this world, walking away from an argument shows weakness.
In this world, it is important to find out everything you can about people you don't know.

Step 2 – Scenarios
The leader should assign each planet a scenario from the list below or invent one for the planet. The unit will then act the scenarios out for the whole group.

Planet Scenario 1 – The group is invited to speak at an intergalactic conference in NYC, but is lost in the subway.

Planet Scenario 2 – The group is at the airport in Chicago trying to decide where to go next on their Earth vacation. Some members feel strongly about visiting Washington D.C. while others want to go to Paris. The flights are leaving soon.

Planet Scenario 3 – The group's vehicle broke down on the way to the hospital in Atlanta. One of the members has a headache that they believe is caused by Earth's atmosphere.

Planet Scenario 4 – The group has rented a house in the country for their visit to Earth. They have discovered a fish tank in one of the bedrooms and instructions for feeding the fish. They have never seen fish before and the fish frighten some of the members of the group.

Step 3 – Mixing Civilizations
The leader should assign a few actors from separate planets a scenario from the list below or invent one. The actors will then perform the scenario for the whole group, being sure to honor the cultural customs of their own planet.

Mixed Culture Scenario 1 – The characters meet on the subway in NYC on the way to an intergalactic conference. They are trying to help each other with subway navigation.

Mixed Culture Scenario 2 – The characters are at an alien singles mixer looking for love.

Mixed Culture Scenario 3 – The characters were the only passengers on a bus tour of Amish country. The bus has broken down miles from civilization. The bus driver left for help and never returned.

Mixed Culture Scenario 4 – The characters are in a holding cell in Area 51 after being interrogated by secret government agents.

Mixed Culture Scenario 5 – One of the characters is hosting a party on his or her yacht to encourage inter-planetary relations.

Mixed Culture Scenario 6 – The characters are stuck in an elevator on the way up to a job interview for the CIA.

Mixed Culture Scenario 7 – The characters are the parents and friends of an intergalactic couple who are getting married at Niagara Falls. The couple rented a cabin for the characters to stay in and they all have just arrived.

Step 4 – Discuss
What was it like creating characters with customs so different from your own? What happened when the characters from different worlds came together?

The fun exercise above created situations where the differences in culture and customs made for entertaining theatre. But the exercise can also remind us of the importance of teamwork in any show. If the director of a play for children intended a world that was high-energy, overly animated and loud and one actor decided to play it like understated realism, that actor would either stick out like a sore thumb or cause the world the company is attempting to create to become difficult for the audience to buy into. You can see the importance of listening to each other and working together to create a unified piece of art.

Terms to Remember:

Company   Suspension of Disbelief

Go Deeper

Improv

One of the things that makes live theatre so exciting is that you never really know what's going to happen. Even though you have rehearsed your blocking, lines, and **business** (the activities an actor performs onstage, such as sifting through the newspaper or repairing a kite), at any given time, you or another actor could forget what you are supposed to do or say, or something could change. An actor must react to what *actually* happens, not what is *supposed* to happen. It is obvious to the audience when an actor is not able to adapt to the reality of each particular performance. A skilled actor will be present in the moment, listening to and reacting to what is going on right then and there.

Let's consider an example. Julian is playing the role of a landscaper named Frank who has just been fired by his boss, Jess, a role that is played by Margery. Their lines are as follows:

Frank:	I've worked my tail off for you for ten years!
Jess:	I just can't afford to keep you, Frank.
Frank:	What about Tony? He's a horrible landscaper.
Jess:	But he's cheap.
Frank:	This is the thanks I get for a job well done. You know, people like you are destroying this country. You have no honor.
Jess:	You're exaggerating Frank. Look, I'll give you a good recommendation.
Frank:	I'll tell you what you can do with your recommendation.

When Julian gets onstage on opening night, he feels extremely nervous. He doesn't remind himself that nerves are his allies. He feels sick to his stomach and distracted. He delivers his first line automatically, to which Margery responds with "I just can't afford to keep you, Frank". That's when it happens. Julian goes blank. He can't remember a word of the scene. Margery and Julian have had many rehearsals off book and have done great with their lines, so Margery doesn't expect this turn of events. But this is live theatre and you never know what's going to happen! Julian just stands there, staring at Margery. What can Margery do? She can't simply jump to her next line, "But he's cheap". That line wouldn't make any sense without Frank's. Luckily Margery has had some practice with **improv** (short for improvisation). In improv, you have to think on your feet, take what is actually given to you and build upon it. Margery hopes that if she can get Julian talking in character, he'll find his way back into the scene. She forgoes her line and says instead, "I know what you're thinking. You're probably wondering why I don't keep Tony."

Julian stares, terrified.

Margery takes what Julian is actually giving her. She says, "You're staring at me like you don't get it. Yeah, Tony might be a horrible landscaper, but he's cheap".

Julian doesn't remember his line but he knows that he is supposed to be angry with the character of Jess. He says the only thing that comes to his head; "I hate you".

Margery hears what Julian says and builds upon it. "Please don't hate me Frank".

Julian remembers part of his line and blurts out, "You're destroying the country! You have no honor".

Margery knows they're back on track. She responds with her line, "You're exaggerating Frank. Look, I'll give you a good recommendation".

Julian says his line "I'll tell you what you can do with your recommendation".

Now the two actors are back where they should be and they continue the scene without another hiccup. Margery and Julian have worked together to get out of a tight spot. They listened to each other, used improvisation (improv for short) and Margery had Julian's back when he needed her. I'm sure he will return the favor when she needs him. This is part of the fun of live theatre. The actors should be proud because they stayed in character and made it work.

If you find yourself lost onstage like Julian, having some skill in improv will help you find your way back to the scene. The important thing to remember in improv is whatever is given is true. For example, if your scene partner says, "you have a bug on your face" you should take that information and build on it, responding perhaps with something like "Ouch! I think it bit me!" or "Get it off, get it off, I have entomophobia!". What you don't want to do is say "no". The scene will turn into an argument and go nowhere. What I mean is, if your partner says "you have a bug on your face" and you respond with "No I don't" the scene might end up looking something like this;

"You have a bug on your face."
"No I don't."
"Yes you do."
"No I don't."
"Yes. It's on you."
"It's not."
"It is."
"Isn't."
"Is."
"Isn't"
"Is."
"Isn't."

What a boring scene! Nobody wants to hear that! If you take what your partner gives you and build on it, it will be so much more interesting . . . and fun.

Let's try a couple exercises to improve our improv skills.

Group Exercise: Word Association Popcorn

Step 1 – Beginner Popcorn
Sit in a circle. Choose someone to start. The first actor will choose another actor in the circle to point to, make eye contact with and say any word that comes to his mind. The second actor will return the eye contact, letting the first actor know that she heard him. The second actor will then choose another actor in the circle to point to, make eye contact with and say the very first word that comes to her mind. And so on. Continue for a little while, letting the exercise pick up speed. Encourage each other to say the first word that comes to mind, without thinking.

Step 2 – Novice Popcorn
Now we'll make it more difficult. We'll have two words strings going at once. Choose two actors to start. Remind everyone to make eye contact and make sure the person they are passing the word to really hears them and receives the word. If they are not sure they have been heard, they should continue pointing and saying the word until the receiving actor has given eye contact and acknowledged them. If you receive two words at once, pass two new words on to two different actors.

Step 3 – Advanced Popcorn
After a few minutes, stop the exercise. See if you still have two word-strings going. If not, try the exercise again, reminding everyone to ensure the person you're passing the word to hears you. If you didn't lose a word they try starting with three words, or even four.

The Word Association Popcorn games help actors listen to each other and think on their feet. It's a great warm-up for improv scenes. Let's try some of those now.

Group Exercise: Song Lyric Improv

Step 1 – Write
Pass out five slips of paper to each person in the group. Each member of the group should write a short fun, funny or unique line from a song on each slip of paper. Fold all the slips of paper and put them in a basket or a hat.

Step 2 – Invent
Choose two actors for the first improv scene. The rest of the group will be the audience. The audience will then decide on the characters the actors will play, where they are located, and what they are doing. (For example the two actors are explorers on the moon searching for a rare moon rock.)

Step 3 – Draw
Each of the actors will draw at random five slips of paper and put them in their pocket without looking at them.

Step 4 – Improv
The actors will begin the improv, remembering to take what is given and build, rather than arguing. At any given time, the leader can say "line" and one actor will pull a slip of paper out of their pocket and say the line that is written, staying in character. The actors must work the line into the scene. The next time the leader says "line", the second actor will read one of their lines, working it into the scene. The scene continues until each actor has used all five lines. The actors must embrace their lyric lines, no matter how silly or out of place they seem.
Variation: The actors can choose when in the scene they want to use their lyric lines, but they cannot read them until they choose to use them. The scene ends when both actors have used all five of their lines.

The above exercise can help actors learn to take whatever is given in their scene and make it work. In live theatre, an actor will sometimes say the wrong line, but the actors must embrace that mistake, consider it a gift and use it to make the scene even better.

Improv is a skill that many actors spend much of their time studying, practicing, and developing. Some actors even make careers out of improv. All actors should be familiar with this skill and spend some time working to become more comfortable with it, as all actors will, sooner or later, find themselves in a situation where improv is a necessity.

Terms to Remember:

Business   Improv

Worksheet

Week Two – Step on Stage

Share a memory of a time in your childhood when you had to speak in front of a group: _____

_____

_____

_____

_____

_____

_____

What emotions does that memory evoke in you? In general, when you consider times you had to speak in front of groups (large or small) as a child, do you have more of a positive or a negative reaction? _____

_____

_____

_____

_____

_____

How can you use past experiences (whether positive or negative) to help you become more confident in front of a group in the future? _____

_____

_____

_____

_____

What exercises from this week resonated with you and why? _____

_____

_____

_____

_____

Does realizing that nerves are your allies give you confidence? Why or why not? _____

_____

_____

_____

_____

What excites you most about the prospect of acting? Why? _____

_____

_____

_____

_____

Week Three

Imagination

Introduction

This week is all about imagination, which is one of the most important abilities you can develop and exercise in your acting training. Actors are storytellers, and although most of the time they can rely on a script, which provides them with facts they need about their characters and situations, the way they interpret and color those facts is personal and deeply influenced by their ability to give life to unique, intriguing scenarios. Imagination helps actors fill the gaps between facts and helps motivate the choices they have to make on stage.

Look Around

Some of the information that actors need might not be present in the script; it might not be considered necessary or relevant to the overall action even though the information might be very important for the actor in order to have a better understanding of the reasons behind their character's actions. It is vital for young actors to exercise their imagination and let their creativity run wild. Remember when you were a child and you spent hours playing with blocks, dolls, and action figures? You invented stories, epic battles, romances, defeated aliens . . . As an actor, you need to go back to that same playful creativity and apply it to your work.

Today's world overwhelms us with stimuli of all sorts and as we enter adulthood, we become very selective in our perception of it in order not to be overwhelmed. Actors need to face the overwhelming reality and absorb as much as possible because it will fuel their "database of experiences" they can access when dealing with roles and situations that they aren't personally familiar with.

Actors need to awaken the child that is buried inside their adult bodies and fantasize about people, situations, and environments. When Stanislavsky was directing at the Moscow Art Theatre, he asked Michael Chekhov to impress him with a scene from his personal life. Chekhov improvised a dramatic scene of his father's death. Stanislavsky was deeply moved by it. Later, he learned that Chekhov's father was actually still alive! This is a great example of the importance of observation and creativity; Michael Chekhov was a great actor, who spent countless hours incorporating everything that he saw and experienced into his work. By attentively watching and interpreting those images and making them his, Chekhov was able to channel truthful grief in such a potent manner without (fortunately) experiencing it firsthand.

Group Discussion: Week Three Worksheet

Read through this week's worksheet (Week Three Worksheet) and discuss the required exercise. Do you think this type of exercise would be helpful to an actor? Why or why not? How do you feel about the prospect of completing this exercise? IMPORTANT: You will need to complete this worksheet by the next session!

Group Exercise: Underscored Imagination Part One

Note: For this exercise, the group leader or instructor will need to provide some various types of music.

Step 1 – Assign
Each actor should be assigned a character and a location (such as police officer at the beach). The group leader/instructor can assign these, or group members can assign them to each other.

Step 2 – Imagine
Get comfortable and close your eyes. The group leader now starts the music. While the music plays, imagine yourself (as your character) in your given location. Imagine what is happening to your character, what you see, what you feel, what you do, who you talk to, etc. Really let your imagination flow, and don't censor yourself.

Step 3 – Discuss
Was it difficult to buy into your imaginary scenario? Was it hard to stay focused on your imaginary scenario and "stay in character" in your mind? How did the music affect your imaginary events?

Group Exercise: Underscored Imagination Part Two

Note: This exercise builds on the previous exercise.

Step 1 – Select
Recall your imaginary scenario from the previous exercise. Try to remember a short part of your scenario that you think would make an interesting thirty-second slice of theatre.

Step 2 – Perform
Rehearse your selected piece without music and perform it for your group.

Step 3 – Discuss
What was it like to translate a selection your imaginary scenario into a performance piece? Did the lack of music have an effect on your performance? Were you able to "stay in character" or did you find nerves getting in your way? Did you find it difficult to utilize your imagination now that you had an audience watching you?

Session Two

Recreate and Retell

Group Discussion: Week Three Worksheet Continued

Before you begin this session, spend some time discussing your experiences with the exercise on this week's worksheet. Share the observations and discoveries you made with your group.

Absorbing all you can from the reality around you will provide you with a sizeable amount of information that you can reuse in different situations and environments (for instance, in a play!). Actors need to allow themselves to isolate elements of reality and place those elements in different situations. How many times have you dreamt of going on a date with your famous actor crush? How many times have you fantasized about winning the lottery and about what you would do with the money? Those improbable scenarios have elements of reality: your famous actor crush is alive and kicking, and lotteries do exist and people win a lot of money!

As aspiring actors, your job is to recreate a believable scenario with circumstantial particulars that aren't necessarily real. So why don't you start by giving yourself permission to fantasize about your wildest dreams in a, sort of, methodical way? The trick is in the details and in the commitment. No one will believe you won the lottery unless *you* really believe it.

Here's an example. Do you remember Anastasia Romanov? Well, Disney had a different take on it, but her real story is as follows:

Anastasia Romanov was one of the daughters of the late Russian Tsar, Nicholas II. She was killed in 1918 along with her entire family. Rumors spread that she had survived (rumors proven wrong by a recent investigation of the victims' remains) and many women claimed to be her. One of them, Anna Anderson, struggled her entire life to prove that she was in fact Anastasia of Russia. Anderson appeared several times in court, underwent several tests and her story proved to be consistent and detailed, yet not sufficiently exhaustive. She died in the late 1980s. The final word on her case was settled with a posthumous DNA test, which determined that she could not be the Russian Grand Duchess, but that she actually was a Polish factory worker struggling with mental illness who had gone missing. Think about how strongly Ms. Anderson believed herself to be Anastasia. Yes, she was mentally ill, but that's not the point. The point is that she fabricated a fascinating and somewhat *believable* story about how she had escaped the massacre. She had thoroughly researched Anastasia Romanov's habits, relationships, and her entire world. She learned so much about her that she could actually retell Anastasia's story as if it were really her own. She fooled many, many people, including herself.

Now, we're not suggesting you identify with your character to the point of mental illness, but we do wish you would consider Ms. Anderson's process. She imagined and fantasized about her escape and she created that story from scratch. She then supported "her" identity with research (with elements of reality). That is what we're recommending you do and that would be the best use of your imagination when it comes to acting!

The following exercises aim to quickly awaken the imagination and further develop creativity, both as individual actors and as members of a company.

Group Exercise: What Is This?

Note: For this exercise, the group leader or instructor will need to provide a variety of objects. They can be common things, such as pencils, scissors, glasses, and so on or they can be more unusual items, such as weirdly looking cooking gadgets with arcane functions (strawberry huller, potato masher, garlic crusher, egg separator, etc.).

Step 1 – Distribute
Pair up and distribute the objects. Each pair should have at least ten objects. One partner per pair should also have a timer (most cellphones have a build in stopwatch. We might as well get some good use out of those pesky, distracting cellphones!)

Step 2 – Invent
Partner A should pick up one object and ask Partner B "What is this?". As soon as the question is asked, B has one minute to invent a fantastic use for that object. It has to be something totally unrelated to the object's real function. B can also demonstrate the use of the object to A. Miming is ok. When the minute is over, Partner A should switch to another object and reset the timer. There should be no pausing in between objects. When A has gone through all of the objects, the exercise should be repeated with B asking "what is this?"

Note: Each pair should exchange their objects with another pair before A and B switch places.

Group Exercise: Body Creations

Step 1 – Create
Divide into two groups. The leader should close his or her eyes and say "go". Each group must try to make one creature or object with their bodies that will be readily identifiable to the leader. Everyone in the group must be part of the object or creature.

(photo credit: Christian Bertrand/Shutterstock.com)

Step 2 – Identify
The leader opens his or her eyes and calls "stop". The leader must then identify the objects the groups have created. If the leader can identify the object or creation, the group gets a point. The game continues and a new creation is formed. The group with the most points at the end wins.

Variation: The leader can assign a creature or object for the groups to create, such as "airplane" or "dragon" and then decide which group created the "best" creation and give the point to that group.

Go Deeper

Imagine All the People

The following exercise is designed to encourage you to rely on your imagination. This exercise will take longer than the previous ones, so take a moment to unwind and get comfortable before you begin.

Group Exercise:

Note: For this exercise, the group leader or instructor will need to lead the group through the fantasy by reading the instructions out loud and taking plenty of time between questions and instructions.

Step 1 – Find a Place
Find a place where you can have relative solitude without distractions. Make sure you have plenty of space between you and your fellow classmates/company members. Sit down and close your eyes. It doesn't matter if you're sitting on the floor or on a chair, as long as you're comfortable and relaxed. Closing your eyes will allow you to work inwardly without being influenced or distracted by whatever happens around you.

Step 2 – Breathe
Breathe. Find your internal rhythm: connect your breath with your heartbeat.

Step 3 – Imagine
Think of someone you would like to be or something you would love to do. Your fantasy must be unrealistic, like being a superhero or traveling in time, etc. See yourself in your chosen role. Imagine what your typical day would be like. (Remember that you are the person in your fantasy and everything you do comes easily and naturally.)
Now imagine all the people that are a part of your world in this fantasy (they don't have to be people you know in real life, but maybe some are there). Who are your friends?
They could be anyone: Superman, Queen Victoria, Michael Jackson, Mother Theresa or an ancient Egyptian Pharaoh.
Imagine something happening, something that involves the people that you are imagining.
Imagine the environment around you: where are you? Is it a familiar place? Is it a place you've never been before? It can be anywhere, but be specific in creating all the details of that space. What are the colors; what are the shades of those colors? If you're outdoors, what's the space like? Are there plants? What kind of plants? What season is it? Are you in a big city? Or in a small town? Is this place in the U.S. or somewhere else? Is it in another Universe?
Be specific. Imagine what you see, what you smell, what you feel when you touch things.
Imagine what happens next, a specific event. Imagine what you do. Imagine what the others do. Focus on the details. Imagine what you say and what the others say.

Personalize your friends as much as possible: if Queen Victoria is your friend, imagine all you can about her. She is your friend; you should know a lot about her. Don't rely exclusively on information you might know from other sources (i.e. your history books). Imagine those things that you wouldn't learn from history books or biographies. What does she eat for breakfast? What's her favorite color? What's her favorite place to go to dinner? Your world has to be consistent with itself, but you don't necessarily have to worry about fashion, social behaviors, and situations contemporary to the real Queen Victoria. Queen Victoria is your friend and she lives in the world you are imagining, which can be the "here and now" or "Pluto 3015".

Imagine the event evolving during your day. Follow up with all its developments and imagine how those influence all the people in your world. Imagine how they react. Listen to their conversations. Enjoy your role in facilitating, triggering, and handling the event. You are the protagonist of your story.

Imagine the resolution of your event and enjoy your "victory" moment. Imagine what that victory might entail. Imagine what you say to the others, and what they say back to you.

Step 4 – Discuss
Come together with your group and discuss the fantasy you've just created and experienced. Discuss how this exercise affected you.

Worksheet

Week Three – Imagination

Go to your local mall. Bring a pencil with you so that you can take notes about your specific observations and your overall experience with this exercise to share with you classmates/ company members.

Find a bench and sit for about twenty minutes. Immerse yourself in the overall atmosphere of the environment. Think of yourself as a sponge, soaking it all in. Is it a busy day at the mall? Is it a lousy day at the mall? Focus on the patterns and trends of people. Where do most people tend to gravitate? Which store attracts whom? Look at the bags that people carry. Do they tell you something about the most popular stores at the mall? What is the general age range of the people present at the mall? Are there more teenagers? Housewives? Is it mostly an elderly crowd? Why is that? Is it a particular time of day that allows only certain categories of people to be out shopping? Is it the weekend? Is the food court busy? What is the most popular restaurant there?

Now shift your focus to a small group of people. Pick people that are close enough for you to see and follow their actions but far enough not to hear their conversations. Follow these people for about ten minutes. Be careful! You're not stalking people, you're observing.

Learn these people. Absorb these people. See what their walking patterns are. Do they have habits? Do they have particular postures? Do they repeat specific gestures? Try to make their postures and gestures yours, but do them slowly. Let your body adjust to someone else's posture naturally; you don't want to make a caricature of someone.

Now imagine what these people are saying. What is the conversation about? What is their personal atmosphere? Does it match the environment surrounding them or does it contrast? Indulge with these people. Create their stories, their background, their conflicts. Imagine the reason why they came to the mall. Imagine what they needed to do here, what they needed to buy, and why. Imagine their households. What is going to happen when they get home? Who are they shopping for? Is it a special occasion?

Now return to your bench and spend some time imagining yourself as part of that group of people. Create your relationship with that group. Imagine meeting those people at the mall, unexpectedly. What is your story? What are you doing at the mall? Why did you come here? What did you need to get, and why? What is your mood? How does your mood influence the group? Imagine the dialogue.

Notes: _____
_____
_____
_____
_____
_____
_____

Week Four

Memory

Introduction

This week we will explore memory. We will focus on rediscovering how important our senses are in our perception of the world, from the larger to the smaller scale, and how the five senses can often serve as portals to our memories and our emotions. We will discuss tips and techniques that will help you with the often intimidating task of memorizing dialog and we will "go deeper" by combining our imagination and our memories of the mundane to create interesting, specific moments of theatre. Let's get started!

Session One

Awakening the Senses

Our mind is truly magnificent and it works tirelessly on many fronts, most of the time without our awareness. We consciously use only a minimal part of our brain for daily activities and larger projects. Our mind stores all the information that we have been exposed to in our lives, and it does a very good job in archiving all of that without our knowledge. If you sit down, close your eyes, and try to remember everything that you've done since the moment you stepped out of bed this morning, you will see that the more you try to remember the details of every action, the harder it gets. Isn't that surprising? How could that happen? After all, not even an entire day has passed!

You consciously select the highlights of your day, but is all the other information lost? No, it's not. Your mind "stores" it. With practice and a greater awareness on your part, you would be able to train yourself to remember more and more details. Of course, remembering all the details of our day on a regular basis wouldn't necessarily benefit us. We usually have a purpose that we need, or want, to accomplish in any given day, and that is what drives our actions. We tend to remember most events related to the completion of that purpose. Sometimes, we are all struck by how easily we forget. How many times have you kicked yourself for losing the car keys or the remote? That's when you try really hard to remember every move you made, and everything you did. You might "retrace your steps" in the hope that by doing so you will find the lost item.

When we "retrace our steps", we are relying on something that goes beyond our normal definition of memory: we are taking advantage of what Stanislavski called "sensory memory". Sensory memory is what our mind remembers physically, through our five senses. Those experiences contribute to building both the memory of our past and the awareness of our present. For example, we remember the taste of pepperoni pizza. We don't have to eat it right now to know what it's like, but we might remember it so well that we crave it and our mouth waters when we think about it. Sensory experiences can also trigger memories of a different kind, for example, when we hear a melody that takes us back to a specific situation: our first prom, or a summer vacation with friends.

Because actors need to recreate situations and experiences in the most believable way, they need to relate to, and find a personal connection with, what their character is going through. Consequently, it is important for actors to take the fullest advantage of their memory and find a way into their experiences, past and present. The greater the specificity of an action the actor is playing on stage, the more effective and honest it will appear to the audience.

Let's try to awaken our senses!

Group Exercise

Note for the group leader/instructor: For this exercise, you will need to have the actors focus on each sense for about fifteen minutes. Some senses might gain the actors' immediate investment;

others might take some time. You should side coach the actors, posing the questions provided below (and other, more space specific questions). Without this coaching, there is the risk that the actors will fall into nothing but routine, passive, walking.

Step 1 – Take in the Environment.
Start walking in the room. Find your rhythm, connect your breath, allow yourself to experience the room as it is. Begin to focus on each of the five senses.

Step 2 – Sight
What can you see? Drink in all you see and be as objective as you can. What are the colors that you see? What are the shapes of the objects in the room? What does the furniture look like? What is the shape of the room itself? What is the floor like? Is there carpet? Or tiles? Hardwood? Does the floor have a pattern? Does the carpet have a specific design? How are the tiles laid down? What is the pattern of the hardwood floor? Look at the walls: what color are they? Are they covered in wallpaper? If so, what is the design? Are there pictures on the wall? What kind? Take your time and remember to keep walking and breathing at a regular pace. As you look at something in the room, consider if you have seen anything like it somewhere else. For example, "this carpet looks like the one in the waiting room of the dentist I went to two months ago". Allow these associations to come naturally, don't force them. If something doesn't ring a bell, let it go and move forward.

Step 3 – Hearing
As you continue to walk in the room, shift your focus to the sounds you can hear. Are there any continuous sounds – like an A/C unit or a heating system? Can you hear anything coming from outside? What is it? Try to isolate the sounds you hear. Is there traffic? Is it heavy? Are there people talking? Can you understand what they are saying? Is there any recurrent sound, like a siren, or a church bell that you can hear? Keep walking, and listen. Can you hear your breath? Can you hear the beating of your heart? What about the other people in the room, are they making noise? What kind? Are you, or anyone else, making a specific sound as you walk? Is that related to the shoes you are wearing? To the type of flooring? Now give yourself some time and try to remember if you have heard any of these sounds before. When? Where? What was the situation?

Step 4 – Smell
Now focus on what you can smell. Is there any particular smell that you can detect? Can you smell paint? Is the air stuffy? Is anyone wearing a perfume? Does anyone smell like fresh laundry? Does anyone smell like they need to shower? Can you smell smoke? Can you smell food? In your own time, begin to associate the current smells with smells you have experienced in the past.

Step 5 – Touch
Now explore the space as if you were only relying on touch. How does the wall feel? Is it cold? Is there a pattern that you can feel? Touch as many objects and pieces of furniture as you can, giving yourself some time to take in each sensation. You might need to pause to really experience each thing. Remember: you are exploring the room on your own. Now isn't the time to waste energy focusing on what the others in the room are thinking or doing. If there is a window, touch the glass. Is it cold? Warm? Can you feel the sun on your face? If you were to identify something just by touching it, would you be able to do it? Try. Did you succeed? Try again, with something else. See if you can find something that feels a way that surprises you. If you do, try to think of why. What were you expecting? When you are ready, begin to associate the feel of the things you are touching with the feel of things you have touched before.

Step 6 – Taste
No: We're not asking you to "taste the room"! Taste is trickier. Sometimes it's associated with smell. For example, if you smell a specific food, you might recall its taste. Taste is very important, but it is usually related to more subjective experiences. At this point, sit down and spend some time recalling specific physical sensations you experienced with taste. Think of a food. Think of

a drink. Think of a condition that left a specific taste in your mouth (e.g., a cold that left you with dry mouth). Do any of these experiences awake memories of situations you hadn't thought about in a while? Spend time thinking about those situations.

Step 7 – Discuss
Discuss what you have experienced. What are the senses that were easier to navigate? Why?

Note: Instructor/group leader: it is recommended to encourage a discussion on what the actors have experienced at the end of the exercise, rather than at the end of each sense. Usually, sight, hearing, and smell play a big role in actors' comments initially, but actors are often surprised about what they discovered during the "touch" portion of the exercise. (Perhaps this is because touch is one of the first tools we use to discover the world in our earliest years, then we tend to neglect it for a number of reasons, including the "please don't touch" mentality that society imposes on us.) Be careful when it comes to discussing the associations. The goal is to let the actors understand the process and how it can help them access their memories through their senses rather than just relying on their memory. They might find that it makes the memories more vivid and present, as if they had just happened. The danger is that they might be surprised with memories that aren't pleasant, or happy. Although actors might choose to use and recreate those situations, the discussion should not focus on the specific content of them. An acting class is not a therapy session!

Session Two

Can You Remember?

Have you ever found yourself asking "how do actors memorize all those lines?" Are you worried about having to remember lines yourself? Maybe you have had to remember lines for a speech or a play in the past and struggled. Perhaps that experience has you second guessing your ability to memorize. Well, there is some good news when it comes to memorization: The more you exercise your memorization muscles, the easier memorization becomes. Also, there are some tips and techniques that will help you with memorization. In this session, we will discuss some of those techniques and tricks. But first, let's have a little fun with a memory warm-up.

(photo credit: stockyimages/ Shutterstock.com)

Group Warm-Up: Memory Shuffle

This warm-up game will exercise your memory, and it is also a fun way to learn facts about other members of the group.

Step 1 – Separate
The group should separate itself into smaller groups based on favorite color. For example, everyone whose favorite color is green will find each other and stand together. Everyone whose favorite color is red will stand together, etc. Try to have maybe six or seven groups maximum. You might have to group some more obscure colors with a more common color. For instance, if your favorite color is "lilac", you could be in the purple group. Spend a few minutes studying the members of each color group, trying to remember them.

Step 2 – Shuffle
When the group leader calls "shuffle", everyone should leave their group and walk around the room, mingling. The group leader will call "stop". Everyone should stop moving. The group leader will call out a color and then choose one person to be "it". "It" must find all the actors with the selected favorite color and pull them aside into a group. If "it" remembers correctly, he or she can continue the game. If "it" forgets, he or she must promptly "die" a dramatic death and lie down on the ground. The leader then calls "separate" and the group separates into their mini-groups again according to their favorite colors. When the leader calls "shuffle", everyone mingles. The leader will call "stop", choose a new color and a new "it", and the new "it" must try to find everyone who with the chosen favorite color. The game continues on until everyone has had a chance to be "it" or until the group leader decides to "switch it up".

Step 3 – Switch it Up
Try the game again with other categories, such as birth month, age, major, favorite holiday, and so on.

Step 4 – Discussion
What was difficult about this game? Was there any trick you used to help you remember who belonged in which group?

Now, let's go over some memorization techniques that you may find helpful. Memorization is a personal activity and a technique that works amazingly for one actor may prove useless for another. The important thing is to try a variety of techniques in order to strike gold. Before we get into tricks and tips, we want to be clear that there is no magic pill that will make memorization instant or effortless. Memorization takes time and repetition. Don't look at the script the day before a performance and expect to be able to "cram" it into your brain. Time is critical. You need time to let the lines and their meanings penetrate your consciousness and become second nature.

Read

The first memorization technique we will discuss might seem a little obvious: reading. Reading the script again and again is the first step you should take in your memorization journey. Look at each word while you read, noticing the words that are unique or unusual to you. Take note of alliteration and poetic sounding lines. Where does the dialog seem rushed or clipped? What language choices did the playwright make that feel uncomfortable to you? Why would the character use those words? Remember, you will be learning the lines word for word as they are written, so you must absorb all that you can.

Wait! Did we just say that you had to learn the lines word for word? Yes, we did. You might be thinking "but it would sound more natural this way", or "I could remember it better if I said this . . ." That might be true, but consider that the theatre organization or school that is producing the play you are performing in is under contract to do the play "as written". Your job as the actor is to learn the lines the way the playwright intended. Does that mean you have to deliver the lines the same way as the original actor who played your role? No. You just must say the words the playwright wrote. Now you might wonder what happens if you forget a line. Do you just stand there silently like a deer in the headlights? No. If you forget your line you improvise something, as we discussed in Week Two. The theatre police won't arrest you for an honest mistake. But hopefully, memorization techniques combined with hard work will render those mistakes few and far between.

As you read and re-read the script, continue to search for new meanings and hidden nuances. Do not read it apathetically. Read it out loud and never use the same inflections. If you use the same inflections every time, you will learn not only the lines, but the rhythm and intonation as well. That will make it difficult for you to be flexible onstage. An actor who is not flexible enough to change inflections and intonation based on what is actually happening onstage will come across as forced, unnatural and/or mechanical.

Read your lines directly before you go to sleep each night. Your mind will process the lines as you sleep. The next morning, as you go about your routine, review your lines. You might be surprised how many you remember from the night before. Try reviewing lines while doing a repetitive physical exercise, such as mowing the lawn or taking a walk. Some actors find that they are able to absorb more information while exercising.

Write

Many actors find that writing down their lines is extremely helpful. Handwriting your lines can give you a stronger connection with the words. Try writing down your lines and then circling the words you believe are the "key" words in each sentence. Which words are most meaningful to the characters? Make sure you are engaging with the words as you work. Don't just copy; read and think about the lines as you write them.

Rehearse

Run your lines over and over with another actor or any volunteer. Grab a co-worker, your mom, your second cousin, or any willing party, and ask them to read the other characters in the scene as you run your lines. If you're having difficulty finding rehearsal partners to contribute as much time as you require, there are a couple little tricks you can try. There's the classic trick of taking a scrap piece of notebook paper and laying it on the page of your script so that your lines are covered. You can then read your cue lines and try to recite your own lines from memory. You can also record the lines the other characters speak and leave silence in the recording when your character is speaking. This way you can "run lines" with the recording whenever you have a chance. There are even some rehearsal apps for actors that work similarly.

Use Imagery and Purpose

Lines that are just words on a page would be difficult for anyone to memorize. If you understand the purpose behind what you are saying (what you want), memorization will be much easier. As you rehearse at home, try using your imagination to link what you are saying to images. You can combine this with your purpose in the scene to really contribute to, not only your memorization efforts, but your connection with the scene as well. For example, you could imagine the reaction your character expects to get in response to a particular line. As you rehearse that line, you can visualize the expected response. Also, use your creativity to find other images to link to your lines. For example, if your character talks about a funeral they attended yesterday, you might create an image of the way the light from a stained glass window reflects off the shiny veneer of the coffin. It's important to be very specific in your imagery and to have fun.

Breath and Blocking

Try rehearsing your lines at home while practicing deep breathing. Remember to relax and release all the tension from your body, focusing on your lines and your breath. As you move into group rehearsals, remember to continue to breathe. Good breathing practices can not only support your vocal projection, but can also help with your focus and your recall. Many actors find that memorization comes easier once they are on their feet rehearsing their blocking and business. Sometimes you can connect your lines to where you are located on stage and what you are doing. For example, "I pour the lemonade when I say this" or "I cross stage left during this line", and so on.

Finally, remember that it is very difficult to undo incorrect memorization, so work hard to get it right the first time; and as suggested earlier, in order to remain flexible in rehearsals and performances, be careful to not to memorize inflections and intonation. You want to be ready to react realistically to what your partner gives you. In the following exercise, we will experiment with some of the above memory tips, in hopes of finding helpful tools that work for each member of the group.

Group Exercise: Memory Experimentation

Step 1 – The Scene
Divide the group into pairs and decide who will play role "A" and who will play role "B". (Use the following short scene or another short scene provided by your leader.)

Scene: *Baby, Bu-Bu, and a Half*
A: She always cries when I walk in the door. She could be having a blast, but as soon as she sees me, it's over. "Bu-Bu". She hollers "Bu-Bu" over and over again until I pick her up.
B: "Bu-Bu"?
A: That's what she calls me.
B: Where'd she get Bu-Bu?
A: No clue.
B: How old is Kayla now?
A: One. Sixteen months. Something like that.

B: I don't get the "x-number of months" thing. It should be one, one and a half, two . . . You know? And you can do the "and a half" until maybe kindergarten and then it's whole numbers only.
A: Yeah . . .
B: Don't you think it's stupid?
A: Then she's one and . . .
B: A half.
A: Not quite.
B: Close enough.
A: Sure. But she's not.
B: Okay then, I guess I'm, what, two hundred and fifty-something months.
A: You're old.
B: That does make me sound old.

Step 2 – Read
Read the scene once with your scene partner. Discuss the scene with your scene partner and decide character names, relationships, location, etc. See if you can remember the lines without looking at the script.

Step 3 – Imagery and Purpose.
Read the scene over several times by yourself. Think about the scene and create imagery and purpose. Think of specific images you can connect to the lines. What does you character want from the other person in the scene? Remember to be specific!

Step 4 – Blocking
Return to your scene partner and work together to decide on blocking for your scene (where you move and when). Rehearse the scene with blocking. Try working off-book (without your script) again.

Step 5 – Breathe
Lay on your back and release your tension into the floor. Focus on your breathing. Make sure your breath feels like it's traveling deep and expanding your stomach as you inhale. After you feel completely relaxed, begin to run your lines with your scene partner as you lie there. Continue breathing deeply as you run your scene twice.

Step 6 – Exercise
Jog in place next to your scene partner as you run through your lines again.

Step 7 – Write
Handwrite your lines, thinking about your characters meaning and purpose as you write them. Circle words you believe are "key" words.

Step 8 – Rehearse
Come back together with your scene partner and rehearse your scene on its feet with blocking and all. Remember to really listen to each other.

Step 9 – Perform
Perform your scene for the class. If you forget a line, use improvisation to get back on track.

Step 10 – Discuss
How successful were you in memorizing your scene? Which memorization tools resonated with you and which did not? Explain. Were there memorization tools that you thought would be useless that actually proved to be helpful when you experimented with them? Do you plan to use any of these memorization tools in the future? Which memorization techniques do you wish you had more time to explore? Which memorization techniques discussed in this session were not used in this exercise?

It's Your Life!

In this session, we will combine what we learned in Session One of this week with what we learned in Week Three: Imagination. This exercise is derived from Uta Hagen's training regimen and it will take some time.

In this exercise, you will work on recreating a physical environment that you should be very familiar with and you should live the reality of it.

Group Exercise: Room Recreation and Scenarios

Note for the group leader/instructor: make sure you have enough space for the actors to play with. You might also need some rehearsal furniture, possibly the usual black blocks, or some tape the actors could use to mark the floor. You will need to lead the actors through the exercise, reading the instructions/questions aloud when necessary.

Step 1 – Breathe
Find a comfortable place in the room and sit down. There should be some distance between you and your peers. It is okay to sit on the floor. Close your eyes. Clear your mind from any thoughts that aren't relevant to this very moment. Connect to your breathing.

Step 2 – Visualize
Now think of your room, at home, or on campus. Take some time to visualize it and bring it in front of your eyes. This phase is very important. Spend time and indulge in all the details of your room. Where is your bed? How big is it? How far is it from the door? Is there a window? Where is it? Do you have curtains? Describe them to yourself. Is there other furniture in the room? What is it? A desk? A chair? Where is each piece of furniture located? Is there a dresser? A closet? Where are your clothes? How is your clothing arranged and stored? Do you have any decorations in your room? What kind? Where? Posters? Art? Is there a TV? A computer?
Be very specific in recreating your room in your mind. How much can you remember? It's likely that you are finding this exercise surprisingly challenging. Despite your room being a very familiar place, it's incredibly difficult to visualize it in detail, isn't it? That's because we take a lot of things that we experience every day for granted. In our ordinary activities, our senses work selectively so that we can prioritize the information we receive and don't get overwhelmed by it all. This exercise, on the other hand, forces you not to be selective. Your brain stores the information, regardless. Now you have to bring it back to life.
Note for the group leader/instructor: Allow the actors to work on this phase for quite some time and make sure to side coach them so that they don't zone out completely. The above step should take about fifteen minutes.

Step 3 – Recreate Space
Stand up and recreate your room in the space. (You'll probably have to take turns as there likely won't be enough space or furniture to go around.) You can use rehearsal furniture, blocks, etc. You can also use tape to mark where everything is, if you don't have enough furniture. You can use props, but it's not necessary. Reproducing the ground plan of your room with tape has proven to be effective, so we would recommend you do it. Take your time and try to get it as accurate as possible. Mark where the door is, the window, etc. Then, when you are satisfied with what you have recreated, get used to this space. Look around. Allow your imagination to fill in everything that inevitably is missing. Get your body acquainted with the real and imaginary objects in the room. Practice entering your room, closing the door and living in the space.

Step 4 – Recreate Life
Recreate a moment of your daily life in the room while your peers look on. It is ok to mime, but be specific!
For example:
It's Friday afternoon. You enter your room with little time to spare; you need to get your bag prepared for an overnight trip to the beach with a friend (choose a *specific* friend). You have a test on Monday (choose a *specific* test), so you will have to bring books. You need to be fast, because you have to catch the train in twenty minutes and your friend will be waiting for you at the station. You probably want to change, you have come home straight from rehearsals and you are wearing rehearsal clothes.
Or
You're coming home late at night after a long trip. You have a suitcase. If you are living with your parents or have roommates, you don't want to wake them up. You are hungry, so you have brought some takeout with you (choose *specific* food). You unwind. You eat your food, maybe read something (a *specific* book), maybe watch television (a *specific* program). Realistically, do what you think you would do in a similar situation.

Note for the group leader/instructor: The original exercise was designed to be longer and to develop over the course of several classes. Here, our goal is to let the actors access their imagination and their memory, exploring their ordinary activities in a familiar place (you could also use a living room or kitchen) and recreating them with the greatest commitment and detail possible. The space they recreate should be accurate and somewhat visible, but it doesn't have to be realistic. They can mime props, or mime dealing with pieces of furniture they don't have on stage. The reality of the items isn't necessary for our purposes: their accuracy in creating them for you, the audience, is.
It is important that the actors see their peers' work, as that will make them better understand the necessity of being specific. There are countless scenarios that you could have the actors focus on. If you have time, you could have them work on their personal scene more than once, so that they can go into greater detail.
We understand that the above exercise might take more time that you can afford in a single class session or meeting time. There is the option of having the actors develop their scenarios on their own during the course of several weeks, and then you could bring them up again when you have time, possibly as a pre-rehearsal warm-up.

Worksheet

Week Four – Memory

Choose a short selection from a poem, play, book, or film that you would like to attempt to commit to memory. Read the text and consider the purpose behind the words. (If the piece is written from a character's point of view, consider the character's intentions behind the speech.)

Without looking at the text, write it down in your own words: _____
_____
_____
_____
_____
_____
_____

Now copy down the text as it is written: _____
_____
_____
_____
_____
_____
_____

Compare the actual text with the text written in your own words. What are the differences? Why do you think the author/poet/playwright choose the words he/she did? Why are the choices appropriate for the character or the piece? _____
_____
_____
_____
_____
_____

Circle the words you consider "key words" in the actual text you copied down (#2 above). Now write those key words here: _____
_____
_____

As you go about your activities throughout the day, recite and contemplate the key words of your selected text. Go back and re-read your selected text at least once per hour. Before retiring at the end of the day, try to recite your text from memory. Were you able to memorize your text? Did you discover anything new or interesting about your text? Did the text have a deeper meaning for you? Reflect on your experience with the text below: _____
_____
_____
_____
_____

Week Five

Open Scenes

Introduction

What is an open scene? An open scene is a scene where characters aren't intentionally defined. They are vaguely named (A, B, C, etc.) and they could be anyone (e.g., A and B could be siblings, lovers, two killers, roommates, or you name it!). The dialogue is also very open and lends itself to as many interpretations as you might want to explore. Open scenes are a perfect way to put into practice what you have learned about imagination and storytelling.

Eight open scenes are provided at the end of this week's sessions.

Do It!

Group Exercise: Open Scenes Part One

Step 1 – Choose
Pair up with a scene partner and choose one of the open scenes provided. (Note that there is an open scene with three characters, in case your group has uneven numbers.)

Step 2 – Create
Decide on characters, a relationship, a location, and a situation for your open scene. For example, if you choose Open Scene 1, you could say that A is a self-absorbed heiress and B is a successful life coach. The relationship could be that B is the life coach to A, and B is frustrated at A's reluctance to pay her bills. B often lectures A about her stingy behavior. The situation could be that, at their last meeting, A didn't pay B for the coaching session, and instead promised to bring the money today. The location could be B's office. Please have fun but be specific. Remember to create a situation and to build relationships with your partner that will read onstage, otherwise the audience will be confused.

Step 3 – Rehearse
Take no more than ten minutes to prepare and rehearse your scene. You can use props, and invent your own ground plan.

Step 4 – Perform
Perform your scene for the group.

Step 5 – Repeat
If time allows, you can invent a new situation, characters, and relationship for the same scene. Do not switch lines (if you are A, remain A and if you are B, continue playing B).

Step 6 – Discuss
Discuss your experiences exploring, developing, and performing your open scene.

Session Two

Switch It Up!

Group Exercise: Open Scenes Part Two

Step 1 – Switch
Repeat the exercise from the session one. Use the same open scenes, but this time switch characters. If you were previously playing A, now play B.

Step 2 – Discuss
Discuss your experiences exploring, developing, and performing your open scene. What did you notice in this session's performance that differed from the last performance?
Note for the group leader/instructor: Feel free to shuffle the scenes and groups according to what you experience and observe. The goal is to make sure that each group develops the scene with the greatest detail and commitment; therefore, if one group is very creative, and another group is struggling, you may want to mix the groups in the way that best facilitates the goal.

Go Deeper

Develop It!

Group Exercise: Open Scenes Part Three

Step 1 – Develop

Now is your chance to flex your playwriting muscles while giving these open scenes some more detail and specificity. Develop these scenes further by adding some dialogue. Start by establishing the situation, characters, and the relationship. (You can use a situation you used in one of the past sessions if you like.) Read the scene as written, keeping in mind the situation, characters, and relationship you've chosen. Read it again, this time allowing the scene to grow and new dialogue to flow. When you are done, go over the new dialogue you added with your partner and see if it makes sense, is consistent, and if it paints the situation correctly, without a lot of useless **exposition** (exposition is background information or backstory revealed through the text). While creating your added dialogue, remember that every scene should have an arch: a beginning, a development, and an end. Make sure you've hit those marks!

Step 2 – Discuss

Discuss any notable experiences or discoveries you've made with your open scenes this week. When did you feel most connected with your character? When did you feel least connected? What were some differences in your scenes and choices from this week?

Term to Remember:

Exposition

Worksheet

Week Five – Open Scenes

Choose one of the scenarios you worked on this week. Discuss your experiences with each of the topics below in relation to your chosen scenario.

Blocking: _____
_____
_____
_____
_____

Memorization: _____
_____
_____
_____
_____

Imagination: _____
_____
_____
_____
_____

Emotional Connection: _____
_____
_____
_____
_____

Believability: _____
_____
_____
_____
_____

Team Work: _____
_____
_____
_____
_____

Eight Open Scenes

In the following pages, we have included eight open scenes for you to use in Week Five. We will also revisit these open scenes in exercises later in the book.

Open Scene 1

> **A:** What's up?
> **B:** Nothing much.
> **A:** You look weird.
> **B:** I can't help it.
> **A:** Why?
> **B:** You know why.
> **A:** Do I?
> **B:** Don't play dumb.
> **A:** I don't know what you're talking about.
> **B:** Did you bring it?
> **A:** I gave it away.
> **B:** Seriously?
> **A:** I thought that's what you wanted.
> **B:** I sorry if I gave you that impression.
> **A:** Too late.
> **B:** Then I guess we are done.
> **A:** So long.

Open Scene 2

> **A:** Hi.
> **B:** What are you doing here?
> **A:** Sightseeing.
> **B:** What's there to see?
> **A:** Look around. Use your imagination.
> **B:** I'd need a lot of imagination.
> **A:** Can you feel it?
> **B:** Did you take your meds today?
> **A:** Hey!
> **B:** Too personal?
> **A:** How long have we known each other?
> **B:** Since I can remember.
> **A:** Exactly.
> **B:** So that's good, right?
> **A:** I 'll let you decide.
> **B:** I'm terrible at that.
> **A:** You'll manage.

Open Scene 3

A: That's so great!

B: Why are you telling me?

A: You are the only one around.

B: I feel special.

A: As you should.

B: Did it cost much?

A: Don't worry about that.

B: What are you hiding?

A: Nothing, I swear.

B: I know that look.

A: You're reading too much into this.

B: It's what I do.

A: Quit it!

B: Oh no, we're going to be late!

A: We can still make it.

B: What are you waiting for?

A: A sign.

Open Scene 4

A: Did you read it?

B: It was awesome.

A: You think?

B: Yeah.

A: What's that look?

B: Nothing.

A: Nothing?

B: Yeah. All is fine.

A: Fine?

B: I mean it.

A: You need to take an acting class.

B: That's insulting.

A: I've got a lot to do.

B: I bet.

A: Really, I need to go.

B: No one's keeping you.

A: Well. Bye.

Open Scene 5

A: I'll take it.

B: Okay then.

A: Is that okay with you?

B: Why wouldn't it be?

A: I don't know.

B: You don't know?

A: I mean, it would be nice.

B: There's a lot to think about.

A: Are you serious?

B: Don't you remember what he said?

A: That doesn't change anything, right?

B: Hm.

A: Are you backing out?

B: Please don't do this again.

A: Hey, you started it.

Open Scene 6

A: What is that smell?

B: I love it.

A: It's very . . . odorous.

B: Sexy.

A: Yeah . . .

B: You have a problem with that?

A: Don't you remember?

B: Just too well.

A: Maybe we should move.

B: It should get fixed.

A: Still, this situation is getting precarious.

B: It does raise some concerns.

A: Yep.

B: Do you want me to address it?

A: Do what you think is best.

B: Sounds good.

Open Scene 7

A: Never mind.

B: No, go ahead.

A: You made it pretty clear.

B: I guess I did.

A: Well. Thank you.

B: So . . . anything else?

A: I wouldn't want to beg.

B: I wouldn't want you to.

A: That's what I thought.

B: You were saying?

A: Nothing, I'm done.

B: I feel weird now.

A: Really?

B: Really.

Open Scene 8 (For three actors)

A: I don't know.

B: Really?

C: I have never seen anything like it before.

B: I don't believe you.

A. Why?

C: So you did it?

B: Of course!

A: Something to be proud of.

C: For sure!

B: What's your problem?

C: Nothing, really.

A: What do we do with it?

B: I don't know!

C: So, why did you do it?

B: It seemed right.

A: I can see that.

C: You can?

B: Of course!

A: It's going to be a surprise.

C: You could say that again.

Week Six

Script and Characters

Introduction

The script is more than a tool for an actor: it's the resource that contains most of the information the actor needs in order to correctly portray a character. It is therefore mandatory to understand and know it in depth, in terms of structure and dynamics. Script analysis is usually part of the actor's initial approach to the part, and it includes a detailed exploration of the script and of the characters, with a specific focus on the character the actor is playing.

How does a script work? Let's look for answers to that question in Session One: What's Happening?

Session One

What's Happening?

When it comes to script analysis, the most important question to answer is also the most obvious one: what's happening? We need to know what's happening in order to figure out what the conflict is, what needs to be resolved, and how each character contributes to it. We will now provide some guidelines for you to use when you approach a script that will help you analyze it and answer that question.

What Is the story?

The **story** is all that happens to the characters in time: it's the so-called "bigger picture", the whole thing. Usually the script provides information about the whole story, but it doesn't portray it. We learn about things that happened before the play actually began by listening to the characters and getting to know them. For example, in *Hamlet*, we learn about Hamlet's father being killed by Claudius, but the murder doesn't happen during the play. Similarly, we learn about Hamlet and Ophelia exchanging love letters, but we don't see that happening on stage. Both these events are part of the story and they are important because they are fundamentals to what triggers Hamlet's and Ophelia's actions in the play. They are part of the characters' timelines, that is to say their biographies: everything that happens to them from the moment they are born to when they have their final appearance in the play (or in life).

What Is the plot?

The **plot**, on the other hand, is a portion of the story. It's what we, audience members, see unfolding on stage. The plot is a selection of events happening in the story that the playwright arranges in order to convey his or her interpretation of it. The plot starts when the play starts and ends at the end of the play.

The events in the plot can be arranged chronologically or episodically. If the events unfold chronologically, the plot is called **linear** or **causal** – casual because the events happen following a cause-effect logic. Most realistic plays have a linear plot.

If the events are arranged in no chronological order, the plot is **episodic**. The most common way to detect an episodic plot is by seeing if the play has flashback or flash-forward scenes. This kind of plot is very popular in non-realistic plays (*Proof*, by David Auburn, for example) and on film and television.

Regardless of its structure, the plot is very important in order to understand what is going on and what part of the story is being told. The playwright, by selecting the events out of the story, inevitably provides his/her interpretation and defines the main characters. If you have to act as one of those characters, you need to discover the playwright's vision of the character and respect it.

A play has a main plot, the one that carries the story, and it might also have subplots, that is to say a series of events that relate to secondary characters. For example, in *A Midsummer Night's Dream*, the mechanicals have their own subplot, and so do Oberon and Titania. Subplots are usually more present in comedies.

What Are the events?

The play presents a series of events, some of which are of a very specific importance. The first one to be mentioned is the **initial event**, or inciting incident, which is the event that sets the action in motion, breaks the stasis, and generates the conflict. Without the initial event, there would be no reason to tell the story.

For example, in *Hamlet*, you could say that the initial event is the death of his father. If Claudius hadn't killed the King, nothing would have happened and young Hamlet would have stayed in Wittenberg pursuing his studies. As we can see, in this case, the initial event happens before the play starts. In other plays, it happens at the very beginning. For example, you could argue that in *A Midsummer Night's Dream*, the initial event is Hermia refusing to follow her father's wish to marry Demetrius, which takes place in Act One, Scene One. The initial event is the only important event that happens in the story, but not necessarily in the plot. It influences all the characters in the play and immediately relates to the conflict.

Another important event is called **climax**, or central event. This event usually occurs closer to the end of the play and it is what culminates the action, with the stakes being at their highest point. After the climax, the play resolves and the conflict is put to rest, thus bringing stasis back. In a good play, the climax needs to be closer to the end, because once the conflict is resolved, there is usually not much left that the audience wants to know.

All the events that happen from the beginning of the play to the climax fall into what it's called **rising action**, whereas what happens after the climax goes by the name of **falling action**. The last event happening in the play is called the **resolution**.

In *Hamlet*, the climax is during the Laertes-Hamlet final duel. It's only at that point that the audience knows that Hamlet's intention of obtaining his revenge is at risk. Hamlet, however, doesn't know of the poisoned sword, and when he is wounded and Laertes confesses to him, he has very little time to accomplish his revenge. That is when the action is at its peak. When Hamlet successfully kills Claudius, order is restored. He asks Horatio to tell the tale, and then Fortinbras enters, claims the crown and restores the political order. Fortinbras' becoming King is the resolution of the play: after that, the order in Denmark is restored.

(photo credit: ID1974/Shutterstock.com)

The events also include the **reversal**, which is a twist in the plot, an unexpected event that creates greater conflict, and makes it even more difficult for the protagonist to get what he wants. For example, in *Hamlet*, a reversal in the plot could be considered the arrival of Rosencrantz and Guildenstern, as they become another obstacle in Hamlet's journey.

Group Exercise: Script Analysis

As a group, discuss and analyze a script using the above elements of play analysis. You can use a script the group is currently reading, or you can use another play that all are likely to be familiar with such as *Romeo and Juliet*.

Note for the group leader/instructor: The actors should begin working on scene assignments in next week's sessions. This could be a good time for them to analyze the script (or scripts) from which their scenes come. If you are assigning them a paper with the script analysis of that play, it would still be appropriate to discuss it applied.

Terms to Remember:

Story	Climax	Resolution
Plot	Rising Action	Reversal
Initial Event	Falling Action	

Who's Making It Happen?

We have analyzed the elements of a play. Let's now discuss the people who are involved and what their roles are in the events.

Every story, therefore every plot, has a **protagonist,** who is the one character who undergoes the greatest change and who accomplishes (or fails to accomplish) the most. For example, in *Hamlet*, the protagonist is, well, Hamlet! Hamlet is the one who is summoned by his father's ghost to revenge his murder and Hamlet is the one who carries the story along, often causing the events to happen. He starts off as a young and very childish man, but during the course of the play, he acquires focus and commitment to his cause to the point that he is ready to sacrifice himself and die for it.

Usually the protagonist isn't quite so easy to determine: not all plays are titled after him or her, and sometimes titles can be deceitful! For example, in Laura Marks' play *Bethany*, the protagonist is Crystal, and Bethany – the title role – isn't even a character in the play. In order to uncover the identity of the protagonist, you have to ask yourself "who is carrying the story?", "which character is the audience most interested in?", and "who is the character who changes the most?" Each play is about someone's journey: the protagonist is that someone.

(photo credit: Igor Bulgarin/Shutterstock.com)

Each protagonist has something, or someone, he is fighting against. We call that the **antagonist**. The antagonist prevents the protagonist from getting what he/she wants. The protagonist is always a character: someone in the play. The antagonist can be a character but it can also be a concept, a group of people, society, an entity, a disease . . . you name it. For example, in *Hamlet*, the antagonist is Claudius: he is the one creating conflict and the person Hamlet needs to defeat. In *Romeo and Juliet*, the antagonist is the hatred between the two families.

All the other characters in a play are functional to the protagonist's journey, one way or the other. They are all called **supporting characters**.

Group Exercise: Short Plays and Analysis

Step 1 – Create
Divide into small groups (four to six actors per group). Each group should come up with a three-to five-minute play where there is a clear protagonist and a clear antagonist. The play needs to depict a clear, yet simple, situation with a beginning, a development, and an end. Try to make the conflict as clear as possible. To highlight the climax, you will freeze and hold the position for five seconds before rolling into the resolution. Take approximately fifteen minutes to come up with your play. You don't have to write a script; you can rely on some improvisation.

Step 2 – Perform
Perform your play for the whole group or class.

Step 3 – Discuss and Analyze
After each small group performs, the whole group/class should discuss and analyze the play. What was successful? What was challenging? What would you do differently?
Were the elements of the play always clear? Was the climax really the high point of the action? Was the conflict strong enough? Were the characters believable? Be careful you are not discussing the quality of the performance and performers, but rather, the structure of the play.

Terms to Remember:

Protagonist   Antagonist   Supporting Characters

Go Deeper

Research Is Fun!

Actors! The script isn't the only resource you should rely on in order to make your choices and build your character. Research is extremely important. It will make your work more specific and lead you to discover incredibly valuable information about your character. It is possible that your director will provide you with some information and research, but directors tend to expect actors to "do their job" and come to rehearsals prepared. The director's research is usually focused on the play as a whole, and not on specifics for each character.

What Do We Mean by Research?

Every play provides a snapshot of a specific time and place. Characters behave and live in certain ways because of that specific time and place. It is thus imperative to investigate the particulars (or the "**given circumstances**") of the so-called "world of the play".

It's always best to start by locating the story. Where is the story set? Learn about the towns, the countries, and the environments in which your character grew up and currently lives. Berlin, Germany, 1940 is very different from New York City, 2014. Characters are just like people: they are influenced by their sociopolitical environment. Research and understand the political, ideological, sociological, and philosophical factors at work in your character's time. What is the economic climate like? What about the physical climate? In what season is the story taking place and what is the weather like in that particular location at that time of the year?

Research everything that affects your character, including mental and physical conditions (Is your character inflicted by a disease? What does that disease entail? Does it influence the way you walk? The way you talk? etc.). All these details might seem useless, but they could provide interesting layers to your character and help you to better understand his or her reactions.

As you read the script, make sure to research anything that comes up and sounds unfamiliar, in particular if the character is referencing specific historical events or figures.

Also, remember that if you are in a period play (for instance, a play written by Shakespeare or Molière), you need to always know exactly what you are saying: Shakespearian English is not the language you currently speak and many words have changed meaning in the course of four hundred years (not to mention that we don't speak in iambic pentameter!).

Group Exercise: Ready, Set, Research!

Note: For this exercise, at least one person in each group will need to have access to the internet.

Step 1 – Prepare
Divide into small groups. Prepare to revisit the play you analyzed as group in session one of this week (Session One: What's Happening?). Ideally, each group will have access to a copy of the text (a digital copy will work).

Step 2 – Treasure Hunt
The group leader or instructor should set a timer (ten minutes is a good amount of time). When the leader says "go", each group hurries to discover the most outrageous, interesting, or odd information about the world of the play in the time allotted.

Step 3 – Vote
Come together as a large group and share the information you discovered. You can vote on which group wins the prize for most interesting research.

Step 4 – Repeat
If desired, you can repeat the exercise using just about anything as a topic for research: another script, a specific time period, a specific public figure, a television show, etc.

Term to Remember:

Given Circumstances

Worksheet

Week Six – Script and Characters

Share your own analysis for an assigned play below. Be certain to include the elements discussed this week and <u>defend your answers</u>. (Ideally, you will analyze the play from which your upcoming scene will be taken, but your group leader or instructor might choose to assign you another script.) Please note, your analysis might be different from another actor's analysis of the same play. That is fine. The important thing is to make sure that all your elements fit together.

Title of Play: _____

Is the plot LINEAR/CAUSAL or EPISODIC? _____
_____
_____

Who is the PROTAGONIST? _____
_____
_____

Who/what is the ANTAGONIST? _____
_____
_____

What is the INITIAL EVENT or inciting incident? _____
_____
_____

Describe the RISING ACTION: _____
_____
_____

Give an example of a REVERSAL in the script: _____
_____
_____

What is the CLIMAX? _____
_____
_____

Describe the FALLING ACTION: _____
_____
_____

What is the RESOLUTION? _____
_____
_____

Week Seven

Script and Scenes

Introduction

This week, we will begin working on a scene assigned to you by your instructor or group leader. Before you delve too deeply into the scene itself, it's important that you understand the play your scene comes from and your character's place in the play. In Week Six, you learned how to analyze a script. If your scene comes from a script that you have already analyzed, you should have a good grip on what is happening in the play and who is making it happen. If your script comes from a play which you haven't approached yet, make sure to take time to thoroughly analyze it, identifying all the elements that we discussed. Also, be sure you understand the purpose that your assigned character serves in the play.

Now, it's time to put some of this knowledge into action.

Session One

The Journey

This session is about making personal choices and gaining a better understanding of your character.

Regardless of whether you are playing the protagonist, the antagonist, or a supporting character, you should consider your role an opportunity to journey into the life of this person. The play certainly gives you enough material to outline your character's actions and motives, but that doesn't mean that it spells everything out for you. You might have to do some digging (research!) to help you fully commit to your character's deeds. This is the time to recognize what about your character resonates the most with you, and what about your character is hard for you to understand.

Every time you are working on your role or on the scene, ensure that you are identifying with your character. You should no longer refer to your character in third person, like you did when you were analyzing the script ("he/she did that because . . ."). Now you should embrace your character ("I did that because . . ."). This process will help you make a connection to the character's choices while still bringing your own personal perspective. You know what your character has to do, but you are totally in charge of the way he or she will do it. The "how" is completely up to you; it is where you can significantly contribute to this fictional person's humanity while giving an outstanding performance on stage. At the same time, keep in mind that in order to be believable, it's imperative that you always stay true to the reality of your character.

You should never judge your character and that's why identifying with the character is so important. Student actors often say, "Well, *I* would never do that, so I don't know how to pretend I would!". Sometimes it is very hard to understand the reasons behind an action, and it can be challenging to play the villain or any other character you have no sympathy for. Yet, only if you rid yourself of judgment and try instead to understand why someone behaves the way they do, will you be able to portray the role believably. Let the audience judge the character: don't do their job for them!

If you are playing the villain, look for his or her redeeming quality. The script will help you, but you will probably have to find your own, personal, reasons. As long as what you settle on doesn't conflict with the script, it's perfectly suitable.

For example, Iago in *Othello* is the one character whose actions are consistently duplicitous and overall mean. He says, very early in the play "I hate the Moor".[1] If you are playing Iago, you have to find out why he hates Othello so much. Is it only because Othello made Cassio his lieutenant instead of him? Or is it something else? What does being the lieutenant mean to Iago? What was the relationship between Iago and Othello before the play began? We know from the play that Othello considers Iago an honest man and a friend, and it appears that Iago gets along with many, but is friends with none. Did Iago consider Othello his only friend and therefore felt betrayed?

---

[1] *Othello*, Act I, Scene 3 v. 385

This is of course a very simplistic evaluation, but it might be a good place to start if you were to play that role. Betrayal triggers strong, irrational reactions in the best of people.

If you were betrayed by someone you thought highly of, what would you do? Quite likely, and hopefully, you wouldn't kill a bunch of people and destroy someone's marriage, but under the right – or very wrong – given circumstances, any human might do just about anything. It is likely you can empathize with Iago, because you probably understand what it feels like to be betrayed. You need that empathy to feed your actions as you identify with the character and play the role. Empathy can set you free from judgment and give you something strong to rely on for the entirety of the performance.

The next step in the journey is to recreate your character's daily life, his/her hobbies, and everything that he/she does when he/she is not involved in the action of the play. Remember: the golden rule is to always go back to the script. We can learn many things from what other characters say about our character and how they relate to him/her.

This step gives you more freedom. As long as what you imagine or come up with isn't in conflict with the reality of the play, it's perfectly acceptable. For example, what if Iago liked music? He does sing in Act Two, Scene Three; so that choice would be supported by the script. If you made that choice, it could influence a lot of what you do on stage.

The more thorough you are when it comes to imbuing the world of your character with your personal touches, the more consistent, specific, and poignant your interpretation is going to be; so take your time to really investigate the play and imagine this person in his/her daily activities.

This approach to your character holds true regardless of if you are playing a lead character or a supporting one. Actually, ensemble roles with very few lines or none at all, require much more creative work on the actor's part, because the play gives very little information about the character. Don't fall into the incorrect perception that Spear Carrier Number Four, with one line in the whole play, is less important than the protagonist. In a theatre production, everyone plays a fundamental role on stage, and the story will be successfully told only if everyone lives in the same reality of truthfulness.

Group Exercise: Character Interview

Step 1 – Volunteer
Pick an actor who would like to be interviewed first, and another volunteer who will play the host.

Step 2 – Introduce
The host will introduce his or her "talk show" and his/her special guest. The special guest will be the actor's character from his/her assigned scene.

Step 3 – Interview
The host will ask the character questions and take questions from the "audience". The actor being interviewed must remain in character the entire time and only answer with "I don't know" if their character wouldn't know the answer. The actor must give answers that would make sense for his/her character.
Note: The purpose of this exercise is to help the actor investigate their character and make believable choices. The purpose is not to try to "trip up" the actor or catch him/her in a mistake. Some of the question asked could include: "What is your favorite dessert?", "Who is your favorite musician?", "What are some of your hobbies?", "Where do you live?", "What does your house look like?", "What does your bedroom look like?", "What's inside your fridge?", "Do you have a pet?", "What's your pet's name?", "How do you feel about your pet?", "Who is your best friend and what do you like about him/her?" How is your relationship with your parents?", "What is your favorite restaurant?", "What do you do for fun?", "Do you play any sports?", "Who intimidates you?", "What are you afraid of?", "What is your favorite vacation spot?", "Why?", and so on. Please be as detailed as you can!

Step 4 – Repeat
Choose a new actor and a new host and continue the exercise until everyone has had a chance
to be interviewed.

The spirit of this exercise shouldn't end when you walk out of the door. You should keep asking yourself
these types of question and include answers and related images in your character journal. (We will
discuss character journals in more detail next week.)

The bottom line is: you need to be curious and very nosy when it comes to your character.

Session Two

Touching the Scene

The first reading of a scene can be a magical experience. Let your imagination soar as you delve into new material and get to know your character. It's important to keep your mind open to fresh ideas and interpretations as you read the script. During the early stages of rehearsal and throughout the rehearsal process, avoid nailing anything down. You want to be flexible and open to new discoveries.

In this session, we will complete several exercises designed for actors dealing with a new script. Grab your scene and your scene partner and let's get to it! First thing's first; Read your scene out loud with your partner. Don't worry about being interesting or "acting", just read to understand the scene and *really listen* to each other.

(photo credit: rui vale sousa/Shutterstock.com)

Exercise: Connection Reading

Sit facing your scene partner with your knees and feet touching. As you read the scene, "lift" the words off the page, making eye contact with your scene partner. While your partner is reading, look at your partner's eyes instead of at your script. Read your scene through twice like this, focusing on connection with your scene partner and listening, rather than entertaining or getting it "right".

Exercise: Subtext Reading

Sit facing your scene partner. Read through the scene as you did in the connection exercise, except this time after each line (or in a pause during your line) speak your character's **subtext** (the underlying meaning behind what your character says) out loud. What is your character really thinking? Take your time, feel free to pause if needed and be sure to speak in first person. Your understanding of your character's subtext will change and develop throughout the rehearsal process, but this is a great way to begin exploring what is going on in your character's mind behind the lines.

Exercise: "Want" Reading

Sit facing your scene partner. Read through the scene as you did in the connection exercise, except this time after each line (or in a pause during your line), speak what your character wants from the other character in the scene, in first person. For example, "I want you to notice me" or "I want you to get off your high horse". Your understanding of the character's wants and desire will develop throughout the rehearsal process, but this exercise will help you begin thinking in these terms.

Group Exercise: Incident Improv

Step 1 – Breakdown

Decide with your partner which incidents or occurrences in your scene are most crucial to its progression. Breakdown your scene into these incidents or occurrences and give a title to each one. Be sure to include the beginning and the end of the scene, and any entrances and exits. For example, your breakdown might look something like this:

> Jill arrives.
> Jill reveals she is angry about Jack's excessive hospital bills.
> Jack tells Jill he's leaving her for a job digging wells.
> Jill apologizes and begs Jack to stay.
> Jack exits.

Step 2 – Improv

After you have broken down your scene, get on your feet and improv the scene with your partner. Make sure to hit each incident or occurrence on your list. Don't worry about getting the lines right; concentrate instead on listening to each other and working through the progression of the scene. If you completed the above reading exercises, you will have some understanding of your character, including your character's wants and subtext. Have fun with your improv, being true to your character.

Step 3 – Improv Again

After you have completed the scene improv with your scene partner, you can perform it for the whole group. Don't worry about repeating exactly what you did previously; concentrate instead on listening to your scene partner and ensuring that you hit each incident or occurrence on your list.

Step 4 – Discuss

What did you discover about the shape of your scene during this exercise? Why did you decide that those particular incidents or occurrences were most critical to the scene? Did you find yourself remembering the lines and working them into your improv? Was it difficult to let go of the script and still remember the structure of the scene? How did the improv alone with your scene partner compare to the improv you did in front of the group?

You and your partner have worked through several exercises designed to introduce you to your scene and encourage you to dig deeper. This is just the tip of the iceberg when it comes to the exploration you and your partner have ahead of you. Take your script home and keep chipping away!

Terms to Remember:

Subtext

Go Deeper

Your Brand New World

Throughout this book, we have frequently referenced the "world of the play". Let's review what exactly we mean by that phrase. Each playwright sets his or her play in a particular "world", whether real or invented. The world is further established by the company. The director and designers research the actual time period and location that the play is set and make choices about which elements they will bring to the stage. Just because something is historically accurate doesn't necessarily mean it will be part of the world of the play. Sometimes directors, playwrights, and designers make choices that differ from the historical reality; thus, a specific "world" is created for each play and each production of that play.

(photo credit: Bystrov/Shutterstock.com)

Actors must learn and understand the values, aesthetics and realities of this unique world and allow that knowledge to influence their approach to the character.

Group Exercise: New World Fairytale

Step 1 – The Story
The group leader or instructor will choose a familiar fairytale or story for the entire large group. Everyone is going to create a short play based on this story.

Step 2 – The World
Divide into small groups. The group leader or instruction will provide each small group with a realistic or fantastical location and a time period (e.g., Egypt in the 19th Century B.C. or Jupiter in 2099). Your group will set the fairytale or story in your assigned location and time period.

Step 3 – Create
Take some time making group decisions about the world of your play. You can do a little bit of research if you like. What are some societal norms, morals, and values? How do people move? How do people relate to each other? What would the set look like, if you had the time and materials needed to create it? Decide how you will execute your scene, staying true to world of the play.

Step 4 – Rehearse
Rehearse your scene, remembering to incorporate the realities of your new world.

Step 5 – Perform
Perform your scene for the entire group or class.

Step 6 – Discuss
What were some of the choices you made for your world? How did the decisions you made about the world of the play affect your script choices and character choices? Did the world of the play affect your characters physically or psychologically? How does the world you created differ from your world in real life? How did each group's performance differ from the others?

When you are examining the world that has been created for your play, it's important to identify what is considered "normal" for characters in that world and how the actions of your character might contrast or conflict with the societal perception of normal. The ways in which a character rebels against, stands in opposition to, or differs from, a culture's norms, speak volumes about the character. For example, perhaps you are playing Jo in *Little Women* and the director and costume designer have decided that Jo will wear trousers for most of the play. Obviously, it would be rare for a young lady in 1860s New England to wear trousers. What does this choice tell you about your character? And what does it say to the audience?

Group Discussion: The World of Your Scene

Discuss the world in which your assigned scene is set. Who are the leaders in that world and who are the followers? In what ways does you character conform to societal norms? In what ways is your character at odds with the culture?

Worksheet

Week Seven – Script and Scenes

Revisit the script that your assigned scene is taken from. Look for clues in the script about what your character likes, his or her activities, relationships, values, and anything else you can find. Don't rush this process! Please take time and really go through the script as if you were looking for a gold nugget. Every piece of information about your character is a gold nugget! Now fill out the information below from your character's point of view. Invent any information that is not provided for you in the script, but be sure it stays true to the world of the play.

Name: _____

Do you have a nickname? What is it and how did you get it?: _____

What is your age and how old do you feel?: _____

What is your social and economic status: _____

What is your favorite color and why?: _____

What is your favorite type of music and why?: _____

What is your favorite food and why?: _____

What is a favorite memory you have and why?: _____
_____

Who do you consider to be your closest friends?: _____
_____

Who do you consider enemies and why?: _____
_____

Who are your family members?: _____
_____

How close are you to your family members and how do you feel about them?: _____
_____

How do you feel about the other character(s) in the scene?: _____
_____

How do you think other character(s) in the scene feel(s) about you?: _____
_____

Where do you live?: _____

How do you feel about where you live and why?: _____
_____

Where do you consider to be home and why?: _____
_____

Where would you go if you could go anywhere and why?: _____
_____

Do you consider yourself an introvert or an extrovert?: _____

Do others consider you an introvert or an extrovert?: _____

Do you consider yourself a leader or a follower?: _____

Do others consider you a leader or a follower?: _____

What animal are you most like and why?: _____

_____

What five adjectives best describe you?: _____

Week Eight

Personalizing Your World

Introduction

This week, we will explore creative ways to make your character's life more personal to you. Perhaps your character is extremely different from you and you are having difficulty relating to him or her. Perhaps, quite bluntly, you just don't like your character very much. Perhaps your character's situation or location is so physically strange that you cannot take it seriously. Even if your character is easy to connect with and as familiar as your twin, you can always personalize further and add depth to your performance. "Becoming" another person is, after all, one of the most exciting things about being an actor. In order to "become" that person, you must explore their world inside and out and solve any mysteries your exploration uncovers. Let's invent, investigate, and eventually come to love these strangers we call characters.

Use Your Senses

An actor arrives at an early rehearsal and his director assigns him some blocking and business for a particular scene. The director tells him that his character will begin the scene sitting at the desk paying bills. She points at the rehearsal props he will be using. For now, the desk is a couple of black wooden cubes stacked on top of each other and the "stack of bills" is simply some scrap paper. Luckily, the actor knows that he can bring reality and life to this scene by using his imagination, his creativity, and his senses. The director says "sit at the desk and pay bills", but this creative actor interprets the direction as follows:

"I sit, running my fingers across the surface of my antique roll-top, cherry wood desk. The surface is smooth, with the exception of a few places where the lacquer has worn and chipped during many years of use. I look at the stack of bills, collection notices, and sale ads piled on the desk in front of me, taunting me. I dread the task at hand. I sigh. The sound of air escaping my throat brings an image to my mind's eye. I see my granddad leaning over this same desk, his huge frame dwarfing the desk chair. I catch the scent of mothballs and Cinnamon Tabaco that followed the old man everywhere. I feel myself smile and taste the saliva in my throat. I try to shake off the memory, knowing I need to get to work. If only my roommate didn't keep it so cold in here. Oh well. I pull the stack of mail towards me, resolved."

Do you see how this actor has pulled from his familiar and colorful sensory experiences to make his time onstage sitting at a desk become more than just sitting at a desk? When you select vivid sensory experiences that you have a real, emotional connection with, you bring a new depth to your acting! In Week Four, Session One, we worked on awakening our senses and we discussed how our senses can provide a way into experiences, past and present. In this session, we'll build on our work with our senses and learn some techniques that will help you incorporate sights, smells, sounds, flavors, and kinesthetic experiences into the lives of your characters.

Group Warm-up: Object Check-In

Step 1 – Object Hunt
Each member of the group should find an object. It can be something you brought with you such as a pencil or a thermos, or it could be something you find in the space. Try to choose an object that is as unique as possible. Everyone should come together, bringing their objects with them.

Step 2 – Explore
Sit in a circle with your group. Close your eyes and use your senses to explore the object you have chosen. Run your hands over the object. Is the surface smooth or rough? Is it hot, cold, or tepid? Are there any sharp edges? Does your object make any noise? What does it sound like if

you shake it? What does it sound like if you tap it? What does your object smell like? What color is it? Does it remind you of anything? Does it have any unusual features? Continue to study your object being as specific as possible.

Step 3 – Adjectives
Choose four adjectives to describe the look, feel, sound, or smell of your object. For example, you might say "soft, blue, stinky, and cold". Going around the circle, everyone should share their four adjectives with the group.

Step 4 – Adjective Introduction
Decide which of your four adjectives best describes you. For example, if Sally's adjectives were soft, blue, stinky, and cold, she might decide that the adjective "cold" best describes herself. Introduce yourself to the group using your chosen adjective. For example, Sally would say "Hello, I'm cold Sally" to which the group would respond "Hello, cold Sally!"

Step 5 – Discuss
After everyone has introduced themselves to the group using their adjectives, discuss what it was like to explore the minute details of your chosen object. When was the last time you paid that much attention to a specific object? Do you think it's important for an actor to have good observational skills? Why or why not? When or in what circumstances do you think an actor might need to use his or her senses for observation?

Actors often have to deal with unrealistic substitutes for things, places, sounds, smells, etc. For example, a character may refer to the scent of climbing roses on a trellis and in reality the roses on the set are plastic. A character might take a shot of whiskey when really the actor is drinking water. A character might be stuck outside during a freezing blizzard when the actor is actually sweating under the stage lights. How do actors overcome reality to make the illusions come to life for not only the audience, but for the actors themselves? An actor must have a skilled imagination and the willingness and self-discipline to do homework. Actors spend time exploring, experiencing, and/or contemplating the actual physical circumstances of their characters. Actors use every one of their senses to make their life onstage seem real. While an actor might not be able to experience an actual blizzard, that actor can feel cold and note how their body reacts to being cold. The actor can look at images and videos of blizzards and people affected by them. An actor might not be able or willing to take a shot of whiskey, but he or she can drink something with a strong flavor and note how their own face, taste buds, and body react. They can interview people about the taste of whiskey, asking questions to discover specifics such as "how does it feel going down your throat?". Actors must be specific in their choices and keen observers of how their bodies reacts to the sights, sounds, smells, tastes, and physical realities of the world around them.

Group Exercise: Substitution Improv

Note: The group leader/instructor will need to provide several items from columns A and B below, or other "real" things and their substitutions for this exercise.

Column A (Substitute props)		Column B ("Real" things)
Bland crackers	substituted for	Sharp cheddar cheese
Wooden block	substituted for	Brick
Pencil	substituted for	Cut flower
Small pillow	substituted for	Old, sentimental teddy bear
Bottle of water	substituted for	Bottle of soda
Folded towel	substituted for	Ice pack
Rolled up sock	substituted for	Baseball
Etc.		Etc.

Step 1 – Explore

Choose one of the "real" things provided by your group leader (items from column B or other items he or she chooses for the exercise). Explore the item as you did in the above "Object Check-In" warm-up. Be very detailed in your exploration, using all of your appropriate senses. How heavy is the object? How does it feel in your hand? How would you use/deal with this item? Use/deal with the object and pay attention to how that feels. If the item is edible, what does it taste like and how does it feel going down your throat? What is the temperature of the item? What does it smell like? Sound like? Does it provoke any emotions? Spend time getting to know your object in and out.

Step 2 – Create

Find a partner and improv a simple scene in which both of you deal with your objects. Rehearse the scene with your partner.

Step 3 – Substitute

Now your leader will take your "real" item and give you its substitute. Perform your scene for the group using your substitute items in place of the "real" things. Use your imagination and your experience with the "real" item to endow the substitute item with the characteristics of the "real" thing. The way you deal with your item in the scene should be believable to you, your scene partner, and the audience. Everyone should be able to easily suspend disbelief and accept the substitute as the real thing because of the way you, the actor, deal with it.

Step 4 – Discuss

How was interacting with the "real" thing different than dealing with its substitute? Did you find it difficult to endow the substitute with the characteristics of the "real" thing? Was the audience distracted by the substitute item? Was your dealing with the substitute believable to you? To your scene partner? To the audience? What was the most challenging aspect of this exercise? Do you think the skills explored in this exercise could be useful to you as an actor? Why or why not?

Have you ever caught whiff of a pleasant scent or repugnant odor, and been reminded of a particular person or past event? Your sense of smell has an almost magical ability to spark your memory and transport you to your past. As an actor, why not take advantage of this ability? You can bring complexity to the lines your character speaks by recalling specific related smells. You can enhance your locations and situations by endowing them with appropriate scents provided by your memory and your experiences. Experiment and find new and exciting ways to use your olfactory power to develop your character and deepen your scenes.

Exercise: Scents in Scenes

Note: For this activity, you will need to spend quite a bit of time working on your own. If there is limited time in your class or group meeting, you can do Steps 1 and 2 on your own before your next rehearsal and then complete Steps 3 and 4 at your next meeting with your scene partner.

Step 1 – Choose

Choose a time in your scene where your character is greatly affected by a past event. Perhaps your character is talking about something that happened in the past or the past significantly colors your character's behavior and emotional state at this particular moment. Now choose a scent that your character associates with this past event. Make sure whatever scent you choose is something that you have access to. For example, if you choose the scent of fresh grass or peppermint or a particular perfume, make sure you can physically access actual grass, peppermint oil or the particular perfume.

Step 2 – Imagine

Collect your chosen scent and find a quiet place where you can be alone. Read over your scene, concentrating specifically on the lines that refer to, or are affected by, your chosen past event. As you read the lines, inhale your chosen scent. Spend at least fifteen minutes reliving your character's past event and adding layers to the memory. As you create and experience the event, keep the scent close by and occasionally smell it as you attempt to connect the scent to your imaginary past events. Repeat this part of the exercise multiple times before your next meeting with your scene partner(s).

Step 3 – Rehearse
After you have worked through Step 2 several times, meet with your scene partner(s) and rehearse the scene. Just before you rehearse, inhale your chosen scent.

Step 4 – Discuss
Did you find it difficult to create specific memories for your character that were connected to a certain scent? Were you able to establish an emotional connection to the scent? Did smelling your scent right before rehearsing your scene help you make a deeper connection with your character? Did your character's memories feel more vivid in rehearsal after conducting this exercise? Is there any element of this exercise that you could see being helpful in the development of your character or the performance of your scene?

Although this session has hopefully furthered your understanding of the excitement of incorporating sense-work into your acting, we've only touched the tip of the iceberg! Your senses are powerful tools. Continue to observe your reactions to the world around you, be specific, and use the information your senses provide to help your characters move from being superficial reflections, towards becoming living, breathing beings!

Create Your Journal

Journaling from your character's point of view gives you the opportunity to explore experiences, opinions and relationships that help make your character the person that they are. Many actors find creating a character journal is not only helpful with, but essential to, character development. Journaling as your character is also a lot of fun! In this session, you will experiment with journaling techniques and get started on your character journal. As you continue adding to your journal throughout the rehearsal process, remember the journal is meant to help you develop a union with your character. What is helpful for one actor might be unconstructive for another. Spend time finding, exploring, and using journaling strategies that work for you.

Coloring the Gray

You have read through your scene and made decisions about your character based on the information given and the lines your character speaks. You have also read the entire play and made decisions based on what other characters say about you, your character's purpose in the story and the intentions of the playwright. You have lifted all the "facts" you can out of the script itself; facts such as "my name is Desiree Stevens", "I live in a small town in Wisconsin", "I am a single mother", "I have a dog named Social", and so on. Still, as you rehearse your scene you can't shake the nagging feeling that you are "acting". Your character feels like a stranger and you avoid thinking too much about certain details of your character's life because they seem foggy and gray. The more you realize you do not know about your character's past life or current situation, the more disconnected you feel.

What can you do? You can begin filling that giant, foggy, gray area with a past and present that will make your character come to life for you. You took a big chunk out of this task in Week Seven: Scripts and Scenes, but it might seem like the more decisions about your character, the bigger the task becomes. Journaling can help! And little by little, piece by piece, you'll create a fleshed out, colorful character that you can slip into as comfortably as your favorite pair of sweatpants.

(photo credit: Breslavtsev Oleg/Shutterstock.com)

Let's look at some examples on how we can use our informed imagination and our character journal to begin to color the gray. You know from reading the script that your name is Desiree Stevens. What's your middle name? You might answer "How should I know? The script doesn't say!" But Desiree Stevens would know her middle name, wouldn't she? So you have to know that too. Here's where informed imagination comes in. You take into account the information you know about your character, your family, your situation, etc. and you use your imagination to make a decision. (We call it "informed" imagination because you must take into account the information you have from the text and not go against the intentions of the playwright.) You write "Desiree Lynn Stevens" on the inside cover of your journal. The first color has been added to the gray. You know your character lives in a small town in Wisconsin because that fact is mentioned in the text, but that's all you know about the town. What is the town's name? How do you feel about living there? Where is your favorite hangout spot? All these things you would know if you really were Desiree, so you decide that you will do a focused freewriting exercise about your hometown.

Focused freewriting is an easy, low-pressure way to add depth to, learn about, and make decisions regarding your character. The following exercise will show you how you can use focused freewriting in your character journal.

Exercise: Focused Freewriting

Note: This exercise can be done with your group or individually.

Step 1 – Choose a Prompt
Read through your scene and choose a prompt. There are endless possibilities when choosing a prompt for your focused freewriting. You can choose any area of your character's life that you want to discover more about (such as the above example of Desiree's hometown), you can choose a relationship with another character in the play, or you can choose a relationship with someone or something that is only referred to in the play (e.g., perhaps Desiree only mentions her dog name Social, but Social is not a character that is ever seen onstage). You could also lift a meaningful line out of the script and start there. The important thing to remember is that the purpose of this focused freewriting is to help "color the gray" and strengthen your union with your character, so choose a prompt that you believe will contribute to that goal. If you are doing this exercise in a group, everyone can share the prompts they've chosen or your group leader/ instructor may assign you a prompt to explore.

Step 2 – Your Journal Entry
We'll use a meaningful line as our example for this exercise. Let's say that in your scene you say to your boyfriend John, "this is just like you. Every time I get the least bit excited about anything, you ruin it for me". At first you think that you understand this line. Obviously, in the past, your character has felt that her dreams or desires were crushed by her boyfriend. But what exactly happened to make her feel that way? How long has she been holding a grudge against John? You realize that when you say this line, it feels empty. Freewriting to the rescue! Close your eyes and begin to create a story behind this line. What causes you to say it? What reaction are you hoping to get from John? After you spend a couple of minutes contemplating the line, write it down as the heading to a journal entry in your character journal. Now pretend that you are your character sitting down to make a journal entry. Read the journal heading you've written and let it speak to you emotionally. Begin to write your journal entry as your character. It's important that you don't censor yourself; just write whatever comes to your character's mind. Let the words and emotions flow out onto the page. Don't worry if it sounds good, if it is well written or if it is "correct". Just put to paper whatever you (as your character) are feeling. Write until you feel the prompt has been fully explored. You might find that this uncensored journaling has revealed more gray areas in your character's life that you would like to investigate.

Step 3 – Read
Congratulations! You have just completed your first journal entry. Go ahead and read it. If you are working in a group setting, everyone in the group can share their entries aloud. You will likely find that your line means so much more now than it did a few minutes ago.

Step 4 – Discuss
What did you discover about your character through this exercise? Did you have a hard time writing without censoring yourself? While completing this journal entry, did you discover more gray areas you would like to explore through freewriting? Do you think that more focused freewriting will help you better connect with your character?

Another great way to "color the gray" is through image collection. If your character talks about her dog named Social, wouldn't it help your lines feel more genuine if you had a mental image of Social the dog? Why not choose a picture of an actual dog and imagine that the dog in the picture is Social. Now when you talk about your dog, you have an image to connect with. That was a very simple example of using images to connect to your character, but you can go further. Let's say you are a playing a middle-aged man who fled his homeland due to war and violence. In your image search, you come across a graphic, realistic painting of a severed hand. You decide to include that image in your journal. You write a journal entry using the image as a prompt. In the journal entry you as your character talk about seeing a severed hand on the dirt street after a bombing. Now, when your character speaks about his decision to leave his homeland, there is so much more behind the lines. Be creative in your use of images in your journal and find what works for you.

Exercise: Image Collection and Journaling

Note for the group leader/instructor: you will need to provide an assortment of images from magazines, catalogs, newspapers, etc. Alternatively, you can have the actors use the internet to find images.

Step 1 – Choose an Image
Look through the provided images until you find one that you believe will help fill in a gray area for your character. For example, perhaps you choose a picture of a tire swing and you imagine it is the swing in your character's childhood backyard where you used to play with your now estranged sister.

Step 2 – Your Journal Entry
Place the image in your journal and spend some time studying it and imagining the connection it has to your character. For example, you might imagine spinning your sister on the tire swing and laughing. When you start to feel an emotional connection with the image, begin uncensored freewriting in your journal. Remember to always journal as your character.

Step 3 – Read and Repeat
Read your journal entry. If you are with your group or class, everyone can read their entries aloud. Next, find more images to include and write about in your journal.

Step 4 – Discuss
What did you discover about your character through this exercise? Did you have a hard time writing without censoring yourself? Did you find it easier to emotionally connect when incorporating an actual image into your imaginary events? While completing this journal entry, did you discover more gray areas that you would like to find images for?

As you journey through the rehearsal process, you will continue to discover gray areas for your character that need coloring. Focused freewriting and image collection are just a couple of the tools you can use to color your gray areas and fill your character journal. Continue to find meaningful lines, relationships and references to use as prompts and keep your character journal close during every rehearsal so you can jot down any gray areas you discover.

Go Deeper

Get On Your Feet

In this session, we will take the skills we have been developing this week and apply them to a scene showing on stage! But before we do that, let's practice applying them to an open scene.

Group Exercise: Open Scene Personalization

Step 1 – Read
Find a scene partner. Choose an open scene to explore or your group leader/instructor may assign you a scene. (Open scenes can be found at the end of Week Five.) Working with your scene partner, decide on a situation, characters, and a relationship. Read through the open scene with your partner.

Step 2 – Journal
Choose two to three prompts that expose "gray areas" for your character in your open scene that you would like to color. Remember, you can use meaningful lines, relationships, or any area of your character's life that you would like to personalize, as a prompt. Refer to the previous session if you need help choosing a prompt. Grab some paper and complete focused freewriting journal entries to explore your chosen prompts.

Step 3 – Sensations
Get together with your scene partner and agree on a specific location for your scene. Discuss and decide on the following:
1. What does this location look like? Be extremely specific! Make sure you discuss objects that are in your imaginary space, what you can see in the distance, etc.
2. What is the temperature and how does the weather or atmosphere affect you?
3. What sounds do you hear? Are they loud or quiet? Are they continuous or intermittent? Do they interrupt your conversation or make you feel the need to adjust your volume?
4. What does this area smell like and how do the smells affect your conversation or mood?

Step 4 – Perform
Get on your feet and perform your open scene for your group or class.

Step 5 – Discuss
How connected did you feel to your character during the performance of your open scene? What aspect of this exercise was most helpful to you in connecting with your character? What did you learn from this exercise that you can apply to your assigned scene?

Now that we've gotten our feet wet with the performance of an open scene, let's step on stage and share a showing of your assigned scene with the class or group.

Exercise: Scene Showing

Step 1 – Prepare
Find a quiet place to prepare for your scene showing. You can try reading through some journal entries, listen to music that helps you connect to your character, inhale the scent you chose in the "Scents in Scenes" exercise, or whatever helps you feel connected to your character's emotional state in this moment of the play.

Step 2 – Apply
Perform your scene for the class, applying the skills you've developed through the previous sessions.

Step 3 –Discuss
In which part of your scene did you feel the most connected? Why? Where do you feel you need the most improvement? Do you feel that journaling helped you connect with your character? Which areas of your scene would you still like to explore through journaling? Which areas do you feel you need to endow with sensory experiences?

Remember that each scene showing is part of an ongoing process. As actors, we never reach the point where our character work is "completed". We can always dig deeper and add more color to our character's world!

Worksheet

Week Eight – Personalizing Your World

Fill in the blanks below from your character's point of view.

When I enter (or when the scene begins), I see _____ which makes me feel _____ because _____. Immediately, I smell the scent of _____ which reminds me of _____ _____ and that memory makes me feel _____. The temperature is _____ and I am _____ about that because_____. In the space, I hear _____.

During the scene, I am intrigued when I see _____ (*name of the other character in the scene*)_____. I am also interested when I hear her/him say, "_____ _____" because_____.

During the scene, I want to see _____.

I want to hear _____.

I want to taste _____.

I want to smell _____.

I want to touch _____.

Week Nine

Survive and Win

Introduction

Part of being human is being in relationships with others. I'm talking about all different kinds of relationships: platonic, romantic, professional, the positive ones, the negative ones, and everything in between. We might like to think that we have no ulterior motives in relationships but in reality we all want something from our interactions with others. Perhaps we want something concrete, like a promotion at work or a second date with a potential lover; perhaps what we want is more ambiguous. Maybe we want to gain a feeling of superiority or we want encouragement or love. The ways we navigate our various relationships and attempt to get what we want from them speak volumes about who we are as people and who we want to be. In life, sometimes we are not consciously aware of our underlying "wants" in our dealings with others, but as actors we need to investigate the scene from every possible angle in order to determine what our characters are trying to achieve and the lengths our characters go to achieve their desires. Just like us, our characters want to not only survive in their situations and in their world, but they also want to win in their relationships.

Session One

What Do I Want?

An important part of an actor's job is determining their character's "wants". These wants have been called many things by acting theorists and directors: objectives, purposes, essential actions, intentions, goals, desires, motives, and more. (We deliberately use terms interchangeably throughout this book.) Don't get caught up on, or confused by, the terminology. The important thing is that we are essentially determining what our characters want from the others onstage. Our characters do not simply speak their lines for no reason. They want specific reactions from the other character (or characters) in the scene.

Exercise – One Word Wants

Step 1 – Memorize
Pair up with a partner. Decide who is Person A and who is Person B and get ready to memorize your lines. These lines will be extremely difficult to memorize. Ready? Here they are.

> Person A: Hi.
> Person B: Hi.
> Person A: Hi.
> Person B: Hi.
> Person A: Hi.
> Person B: Hi.

You think you can handle that?

Step 2 – Simple Secret Something
Each partner should choose a simple secret something that they want from the other. Don't tell your partner what you want from them! Make sure what you want is simple and it is **something that you can get from your scene partner.** Don't pick something impossible to achieve. Likewise, don't pick something that you do not need the other person for. What you are trying to achieve must be possible (although it can be difficult) and you must be able to look to your partner to see if you are getting what you want. For example, you might want a kind smile or warm hug. You might want to intimidate them or impress them. All of those things are possible and you need your scene partner to get what you want in each of those examples.

Step 3 – Perform
You and your scene partner will now perform the scene. Each partner will try their hardest to get what they want from the other character in the scene. Important! You must not change the lines. You can only use the lines given to you by the playwright.

Step 4 – Reveal and Discuss

What were you trying to gain from your scene partner? Were you able to look to your scene partner to see if you were getting what you wanted? Was it easy to achieve your goal or did you have to keep working harder? Were the scenes more interesting when the characters had to work hard to get what they wanted?

In the above exercise, you might have uncovered some interesting revelations about choosing your character's "wants". You may have discovered one or more of the following facts:

1. The scene is more interesting when both characters' wants (at least sometimes) oppose each other.
2. The scene is more interesting and realistic when a character is trying to get something from the other character(s) in the scene, rather than trying to show something to the audience.
3. It's hard for a character to be invested in a "want" that the character doesn't believe to be possible.

Remembering these three facts and applying their lessons to our work onstage can make an otherwise dull, unbelievable performance stellar and real. Let's examine them further.

Fact #1: The Scene is More Interesting when Both Characters' Wants (At Least Sometimes) Oppose Each Other.

Usually, playwrights write about moments of conflict; one character's desires oppose the other's. If there are no opposing goals or "wants", the scene may become rather boring. On the surface, both characters' lines might seem in agreement; for example:

Person A: "I think we should break up."
Person B: "I was just about to say the same thing."
Person A: "Fantastic."
Person B: "I wish you the best."
Person A: "You too."

Person A and Person B could both say that their goal is to end the relationship with the other without causing pain. The audience watches the scene, falls asleep and misses the rest of the play.

Let's look at our example scene again. This time the actors choose different "wants" for their characters. Person A decides that her character wants to wheedle a confession of love from her partner. Person B chooses that his character wants to demean his partner. Now read the scene again. The lines have not changed, but the decisions the actors made about their character's "wants" change the subtext and make the scene much more exciting.

Sometimes a scene will go from a place where both character's "wants" oppose each other, to a place where the "wants" are similar or vice versa. This can also make for an interesting, dynamic scene.

Fact #2: The Scene is More Interesting and Realistic When Your Character is Trying to Get Something from the Other Character(s) in the Scene, Rather than Trying to Show Something to the Audience.

It's easy to accidentally make the scene about what you are showing, rather than what you are trying to get from the other person. When you do this, you are depriving your scene of a real, in-the-moment relationship between characters and you are depriving yourself of the thrill of coming alive and being present onstage; your acting may seem self-conscious, or "showy". Although the audience might not be able to pin down exactly what is wrong with the acting, it won't be as believable or as moving to them.

Let's use the short scene above for an example. Person B decides what he wants is to "be sad". When Person A says she wants to break up, he doesn't need anything from her, he just has to stand onstage and look sad. You might think this will gain the most sympathy from the audience, especially if you can work up some real tears, but remember that audience members are intelligent and they will usually be able to tell when they are being manipulated. Let's say instead of wanting simply to "be sad" Person B chooses something that he wants from Person A. Perhaps, because he loves Person A, he wants to reassure her that he's okay. He wants something from her. He wants her to be reassured. He's still sad, but the now the audience sees a character fighting through his own sorrow and focusing on his partner. It's not about the audience, it's about the relationship between the characters onstage. The audience members are free to mourn, cry, love, and identify with the characters in the play because they are not feeling manipulated.

Fact #3: It's Hard to for a Character to Be Invested in A "Want" That the Character Doesn't Believe to be Possible.

This fact is pretty straightforward. If your character doesn't believe what they are trying to achieve is possible, they won't work hard to achieve it. Even if you, as the actor, know that your character fails in the end, you must not let your *character* know that. Your character has to believe he can get what he wants from the others in the scene and fight to win!

Your Scene Score

A scene score is a tool an actor creates to interpret what his character is doing during a scene and when and why he's doing it. The scene score helps the scene become more active and also helps the actor explore the subtext. Since each actor is different, what each actor includes in his scene score can look different as well. Scene scores might note the character's "wants", obstacles that stand in the way of the character's "wants", emotional shifts and/or topic changes, tactics or strategies that the character employs to get what he wants, and anything else the actor finds helpful. In this next exercise, you will begin the work of scoring your scene by notating the character's "wants" and when those "wants" change.

Exercise: Starting your Scene Score

Note: This is an exercise that should be done individually, without the help of your scene partner. In real life, we don't have definitive knowledge of what the people we deal with want from us, so the scene can be more life-like and active if you are not 100% sure what your scene partner is trying to get from you.

Step 1 – Think
Collect your script and a pencil. Be sure to use a pencil, because what you believe your character is fighting for might change throughout the rehearsal process, as you learn more about your character and deepen your connection to him/her. Read the scene and think about what your character is wanting from the other character(s). What does your character want when the scene begins? Does this "want" change throughout the scene?

Step 2 – Simplify
Make sure to look at each "want" and see if you missed the deeper reason behind the "want". This is especially important if you find that your "wants" change with every line or two. If you ask yourself, "why do I want that?" you might find that your character has a more significant desire that carries him or her throughout much of the scene. Always look for the deep, underlying reaction you want from the other person in the scene.

Step 3 – Write and Revisit
Write in your script your "want" or "wants". Be sure to note where one "want" subsides and a new "want" takes its place (know that it is possible that your character is fighting for a single

thing throughout the scene. He or she might not change what they want, he/she might simply change how they go about getting it. We'll discuss this further in the next session). Throughout the rehearsal process, continue to be open to change if you discover something new, or if the "wants" you've chosen just aren't working for you as an actor.

Knowing what your character wants and fighting hard to get it makes a scene go from dull and lifeless to exciting and alive. Focusing on getting what you from the others onstage makes your acting go from surface and "showy" to believable and "in-the-moment". As an actor, fighting to win is fun!

Session Two

How Do I Get It?

When you find a hundred people that all want the same thing, you might have found a hundred different ways to go about getting it.

You've investigated what your character wants from the others onstage, but how he or she goes about getting what he/she wants gives you a great insight into who he/she is. Your character employs different strategies or tactics, or actions (we deliberately use these terms interchangeably throughout this book, as you will hear them all spoken in the theatre world) to achieve goals. These strategies are what really bring variety to your scene. When your character determines that one strategy isn't working, he tries something new. Just like in real life, he does not keep trying the thing that isn't working; instead, he tries a fresh way to get what he wants. Changing strategies or tactics based on the response of the others onstage keeps a scene dynamic and interesting for actors and also for the audience.

Exercise: Tactic Phone Call

Step 1 – Create
Think of a person in your life that you might make a phone call to. Now think of something that you want from them (it can be something you want in real life or you can invent something; just make sure it's believable). Decide on three tactics, or three different strategies, you are going to use to try to get what you want. Make sure the tactics are very different from each other.

Step 2 – Perform
Perform your phone call for your group or class. Imagine that the person on the other end of the phone line is not giving you what you want. After you try one tactic and discover it's not working, switch to another tactic. Continue your phone conversation until you have exhausted all three tactics, and then end the phone conversation. You can decide whether to end your phone call with a victory or a defeat.

Step 3 – Discuss
Did you find it difficult or easy to think of three different ways to go about getting what you wanted? Which changes in tactic did the actor and/or audience find most interesting and why?

Make sure you are using active verbs to describe your character's tactics and make sure the verbs you choose speak strongly to you and are exciting for you as the actor to play. Also, remember that switching tactics should add variety to your scene, so instead of choosing an active verb that is similar to the previous active verb, choose something with a different flavor that can spice up your scene. For example, let's compare the tactic choices of three different actors. Let's say that all three actors are working on the role of Samarina, whose sister is being held captive by King Milo, the villain.

Actor A first tries <u>to convince</u> King Milo to let her sister go; next, she tries <u>to persuade</u> King Milo; and finally, she tries <u>to counsel</u> King Milo to free her sister.

Actor B tries a different approach. First, she tries <u>to demand</u> he set her sister free; next, she tries <u>to threaten</u> him to free her sister; and finally, she tries <u>to bully</u> him into releasing her little sister.

Actor C tries <u>to seduce</u> King Milo; next, she tries <u>to threaten</u> him; and finally, she tries <u>to beg</u>, all in an effort to get him to let her sister go.

It's important to note that each of these actors is working off the same script with the same lines. The only thing that changes is the way that they deliver the lines. Actor A's method comes across rather dull. Her action/strategy/tactic choices not only lack variety, but they also aren't very exciting to play. Convincing, persuading, and counseling might be okay choices for limited moments in a script, but they are not ideally compelling and they are so similar that audience might not notice any change in tactic at all. Actor B has the right idea as far as choosing interesting tactics that are exciting to play; however, she falls into the same trap as Actor A, insofar as her tactic choices (to demand, to threaten and to bully) are similar to each other, resulting in limited variety. Actor C's choices (to seduce, to threaten, and to beg) result in a more exciting and interesting version of the scene. Her strategies are very different from each other and they are captivating for actor and audience alike.

Group Exercise: Strategy Switch-Up

Note: For this exercise, the group leader or instructor will need to provide at least twenty sheets of paper and a bell or other noise maker.

Step 1 – Write
As a group, think of twenty or more strategies/actions/tactics and write each one on a piece of paper. Here are some examples of tactics you might use: to admonish, to beseech, to defy, to destroy, to enkindle, to frighten, to patronize, to pester, to push, to validate.

Step 2 – Sort
Divide your tactics into two piles. The first pile will include strategies you consider to be more heavy handed, or harsher (we will call these the "heavy" tactics). The second pile will be made up of gentler or craftier strategies (we will call these the "light" tactics). For example, the first pile might include: to admonish, to defy, to destroy, to frighten, and to push, while the second pile might include: to patronize, to beseech, to pester, to validate, and to enkindle.

Step 3 – Act
Choose one pair of scene partners who would like to go first, one bell ringer, and someone to hold up the strategy signs from each pile. The scene partners should get up before the group and begin their scene. At any moment in the scene, the bell ringer can ring the bell and the sign holder raises a strategy sign. Whichever actor is speaking should change their current strategy/tactic to match the strategy on the sign. The bell ringer continues to choose moments throughout scene to ring the bell. Every time the bell is rung, the sign holder raises a new strategy, alternating between the "heavy" pile and the "light" pile. Note: even if the actor believes that the strategy doesn't "make sense" for the character, the actor must embrace it and play it to the best of their ability.

Step 4 – Repeat
Try it with a new pair of actors!

Step 5 – Discuss
Did you discover any tactics that worked for your scene that you would have never tried otherwise? Which strategies were the most difficult to play? Which were the easiest? Which were the most enjoyable? What was it like switching between the "heavy" strategies and the "light" strategies? Did you notice new variety in the other actors' scenes?

Exercise: Adding to Your Scene Score

Note: This is an exercise that should be done individually.

On the margins of your scene, make a list of actions you would like try at your next rehearsal. Let this be a dynamic list that you change and develop throughout your rehearsal process. If you find a tactic that is especially exciting and really works for you as your character, make a note of it on your list.

Go Deeper

Raising the Stakes

If the scene you are playing doesn't "feel" right, it might be because the conflict isn't surfacing enough and because you are too comfortable in your role. By raising the stakes, you will be able to acquire a greater connection to what the character needs.

"Raising the stakes" includes figuring out what might happen if you don't get what you want in the scene, and overall, in the play. Sometimes the script offers you enough material to effectively figure out what will happen to your character if he/she doesn't win, but some personal work might be necessary to fill in the blanks.

There are several ways you can go about raising the stakes. One of them is to use the "magic if", which is one of the elements introduced by Stanislavski. The "magic if" helps the actor make a personal connection to the character. The actor approaches the character by asking himself/herself: "What would I do if I were in those circumstances?" As you can imagine, this approach works best if the actor has gathered the greatest amount of information possible about the given circumstances of the his or her character.

The "magic if" only works if the actor allows himself to realistically imagine how the given circumstances of the character and of the play would affect his own actions. Usually, the greatest resistance comes from the fact that actors think: "but I have never been in that situation, so I don't know what I would do" or "but I would never kill somebody", or "I would never do what he does". One of Stanislavski's actors, Eugene Vakhtangov, probably gave the best definition of "magic if", so here it is: the "magic if is what I need to do in order to do what the character does in these circumstances". So, if you turn it into a question, that would be: "What do I have to do in order to do what the character does in these circumstances?". The answer to that question is very personal, and it will be part of your own research, which you don't necessarily have to share.

Let's try an exercise aimed to help actors work on "raising the stakes".

(photo credit: Guryanov Andrey/Shutterstock.com)

Exercise: Raising the Stakes

Step 1 – The Scenario
Find a scene partner. Decide who will play the traveler and who will play the customer service agent. The group leader or instructor should read the following scenario:
The traveler is traveling from Charleston to Boston. There were no direct flights, so he/she had to connect in Atlanta. The first flight was late, so he/she lost the connection in Atlanta. The traveler is at the airline customer service desk trying to get on the next flight, but it's full and it's the last one of the day. The customer service agent tells the traveler that he/she can be on a flight leaving tomorrow. The traveler throws a tantrum.

Step 2 – The Dialogue
Imagine the dialogue. (You might want to write it down, or you can improvise.)

Step 3 – Take One
Put it on its feet and play with it.

Step 4 – Raise the Stakes
Now, try to raise the stakes and try to see what's happening with the characters. First, focus on the actor who plays the traveler. Why is he/she in such a hurry to get to Boston? Why does he/she throw a tantrum? Here, you don't have the script to help you identify your given circumstances, so you will have to come up with your own situations, backstory and **internal monologue** (that is, the thoughts that are running through your character's mind and informing your choices).

What would your internal monologue be? For example, it could be something like:

> "If I don't get to Boston tonight, my father will think I'm a loser who can't get the airline do what I ask after they made a mistake. If my father thinks I'm a loser, he will stop trusting me. If he stops trusting me, he won't pay for my college tuition any longer. If he stops paying for my college tuition, I will have to stop doing what I love and I will have to look desperately for a job in order to pay my rent. If get trapped in a job I hate, I won't be happy. So if <u>I don't get to Boston tonight, I will lose my chance at happiness</u>."

Take your time to really focus on what will happen to you if you don't get what you want. Allow your imagination to guide and inform your scene and the dialogue.

Step 5 – Take Two
Perform the scene again, with the stakes raised for the traveler.

Step 6 – Raise the Stakes Again
Now, raise the stakes again like you did in Step 4, but this time focus on the customer service agent.

Step 7 – Take Three
Perform the scene again, with the stakes raised for both the traveler and the customer service agent.

Terms to Remember:

Internal Monologue

Worksheet

Week Nine – Survive and Win

Look at the list of 21 tactics/strategies/actions provided. Put them in the "heavy" or "light" column depending on how you interpret them. (Note that some tactics could be considered heavy or light depending on how they're played by the actor, so you might decide to include some tactics in both columns.)

TO HEAL	TO RALLY	TO DRIVE
TO TRIVIALIZE	TO BRIBE	TO SCOLD
TO PROVOKE	TO ENCOURAGE	TO COAX
TO CONDEMN	TO SMOTHER	TO TAUNT
TO LURE	TO ENFLAME	TO FLATTER
TO INTIMIDATE	TO TERRIFY	TO SHOCK
TO PUSH	TO REASSURE	TO DEMOLISH

Heavy

_____

_____

_____

_____

_____

_____

_____

_____

_____

_____

_____

_____

_____

_____

_____

_____

_____

_____

Light

_____

_____

_____

_____

_____

_____

_____

_____

_____

_____

_____

_____

_____

_____

_____

_____

_____

_____

Now add a few of your own actions to each column. Circle several tactics in each column that you think you might like to try in your scene.

Week Ten

Listening

Introduction

In Week Two, we began our discussion about listening and reacting to what's actually given onstage. This week, we will go farther with our work on the topics of trust, reacting to each other, reacting to the environment, and listening. As actors, we need to learn to listen, not only with our ears, but with our entire beings.

Session One

You Are Not Alone

This session emphasizes the importance of shifting the focus to your partners when you are on stage. You have probably heard it before: acting is mostly reacting. Let's examine what that really means.

When you are playing a character in a play, you probably have a lot of information and ideas about what your character wants and what he or she needs to do in order to accomplish it. Blocking gives you business to do on stage and cues to respect. By the time you hit opening night, and to some extent even throughout the rehearsal process, you should be fairly confident about what you are "supposed to do" and what "is expected of you" from the director and in some cases, the playwright.

So, is that all?

No, we're afraid it's not, which is one of the reasons why acting is such a multifaceted, ongoing, and ever changing experience! There are so many variables that come to play when you are part of a live performance. We mentioned in Week One that Theatre is a unique art form, because it's live and it changes with every performance. The script doesn't change, the blocking might be the same, the director's concept may stay consistent, but the given circumstances of the ensemble, that is, the cast, the audience, and the environment as a whole, make for a completely different situation that you can't be oblivious to.

Sanford Meisner, one of the most important acting instructors, urged his actors to always "be in the moment", which means allow yourself the luxury of living the circumstances of the character you are playing here and now, as if the action is unfolding for the first time ever. It seems like such an easy thing to do, doesn't it? Unfortunately, it's easier said than done!

Since the moment you received your script, you worked hard to memorize everything: lines, blocking, stage business, and whatnot. In your mind, everything should function like clockwork, because that's how the story is supposed to be told. We're not denying the fundamental importance of rehearsals and hard work, mind you! Yet, when you have reached a higher level of confidence in your role, you tend to isolate yourself within the story and simply become an automated part of a mechanism, thus losing the connection to your inner life and, most importantly, to the present situation: the right here, right now.

You are not alone on stage. Even if you have very few lines, there is always a reason that the playwright put you there. As challenging as it might be, you have to find that reason and you have to really "be present". That's why listening is so important. You need to allow yourself to focus on the scene that is developing on stage and be open to react to whatever happens. Situations change, conditions do too: your partner in the scene might resent some physical or emotional distress, and that might influence his/her performance. That's not necessarily a bad thing, but you have to receive and react to what your partner gives you, not to what you think he/she should have given to you. You have learned from your experience with open scenes that the same line can acquire so many meanings and can contain countless nuances. So, even if the material stays the same, that is to say the lines, the blocking, the business, etc., your connection to it needs to adjust according to whatever you are receiving in the moment.

The beauty of a live performance involves the element of the unpredictable. A "mistake", or an accident, can always happen, but as you know, the show must go on (unless the accident is so grave that it necessitates stopping the show). If you continue to pursue theatre, you will hear actors and directors tell the most entertaining stories about mistakes and technical misadventures, but you will frequently hear how those unfortunate coincidences actually turned out to add a little something to the show.

Kiara Pipino cannot pass up the opportunity to share a couple of her stories regarding this matter.

"One of my first directing jobs was directing a comedic original piece on Greek classic characters (Aegisthus, Clytemnestra, Agamemnon, Electra, Orestes, and Cassandra) for a summer theatre festival in an open air venue. I knew most of the actors and I had a wonderful time rehearsing. The piece featured all characters breaking the fourth wall and telling their story to the audience. At one point, Clytemnestra, Agamemnon and Aegisthus were on stage and Cassandra was to enter. Her line as she entered was "I can see. . . . I can see. . . .". The moment she said the line, the electricity in the entire area (not just on stage) went off.

I would call that a major technical failure, wouldn't you? As a director, I was panicking and cursing in seven languages in the booth, while I desperately looked for a flash light . . . like I could, I don't know, use it as a follow spot. . . .

In the meantime, on stage, my actors had just the right reaction. The actor playing Aegisthus said out loud 'They told us you would bring bad luck', and Clytemnestra started chasing Cassandra, bumping into a lot of stuff and causing the audience to laugh wholeheartedly.

I can't really tell how long the blackout lasted. I would say thirty seconds tops. Probably the longest thirty seconds of my life as a director. Then the lights came back on and my actors reacted to it, they thanked Zeus and resumed their scene. The audience didn't even notice the mistake. They all thought the blackout had been intentional. So we kept the blackout for the following performances!

Another time, I was directing a comedy. One of the characters had to fall asleep on the couch, and sleep through the scene, unnoticed by the others. The character suffered from narcolepsy, and all the other characters in the play made fun of her because of that. Well, as it turned out, my actor actually fell asleep during the scene (she later said the couch was so comfortable). She slept through the scene and way into intermission. She woke up during intermission. She looked around. She realized what had happened and quickly made the choice to fall asleep again and wake up after intermission, as she was supposed to be awake in the opening scene of Act Two. The audience didn't know that wasn't supposed to happen. The stage manager and the other cast members freaked out and I. . . . well . . . I ordered a glass of wine and had coffee delivered to my actor's dressing room."

These examples give you an idea of how a problem can turn out to become an opportunity thanks to the actors staying in the moment. In the first situation, the blackout could have caused the actors to panic like Kiara did, because that wasn't supposed to happen. They could have just stopped the show and waited for the lights to come back on, making it crystal clear that that wasn't part of the show. Instead, they took advantage of the situation and turned it into a successful moment.

In the second example, the situation was a bit trickier. The actor who fell asleep clearly lost control of the situation, but she recovered brilliantly and without breaking character. The other actors on the other hand had a hard time during intermission. The scene ended with a blackout, which was there to facilitate the exit of the actors and a prompt intermission. They only realized that she had stayed on stage when house lights came back up. They knew she was very tired: her baby had kept her up all night. But what could they do? Does the storytelling stop during intermission? Should the stage manager have awoken her? That would have broken the world of the play and revealed the mistake. After some discussion, which Kiara was a part of, they concluded that they would let her sleep and wake her up, as if it were scripted, in the opening scene of Act Two.

As you can see, these two examples pointed out once again the importance of ensemble work and of listening, on stage. When you are part of a show, you become part of a new family and you should function like one. You are all serving the script and telling the story. You have to be there for your partner if something unexpected happens. You also know that they will be there for you if and when you need help.

In order to apply and practice what we have just learned, you don't have to wait for some accident or mistake to happen during rehearsals or during a performance! Let's work on some exercises that aim at helping you listen and react.

Group Exercise: Paraphrase and Morph

(This exercise is similar to previous exercises, but with a different focus.)
Note for the group leader/instructor: For this exercise, you will need to assign the actors scenes, and divide them accordingly. You can use the scene that they've been working on, but it's important that the actors are not yet off book. For the purpose of this exercise, it's not advisable to use the open scenes. Make sure you observe the groups closely. You want the actors to really receive and react organically. The risk is that they will get carried away by the game and lose track of the stakes.

Step 1 – Discover
Read your scene with your partner(s). Take your time to understand what is going on in the scene. What do you want? How badly do you want it? What's at stake? What is the best possible outcome for you? Discuss all this within your group. If you're using a scene you've worked on previously, you should already know the answers to these questions and you can skip ahead to the next step.

Step 2 – Read
Read the scene a few more times so that you get the idea of how it develops and unfolds. This should take no longer than ten minutes. There is no need to attempt memorization.

Step 3 – Do It
Put the scene on its feet! Leave the scripts behind, and go for it! Yes: you should paraphrase. The important thing is to make sure that you are pursuing your objective, playing your actions and that, of course, you stick to the given circumstances of the scene. Try to respect the length of the scene and improvise the dialogue. Make sure to keep the stakes high and stay focused on your partner.

Step 4 – Develop It
Rehearse the scene a couple of times. You don't want to get too comfortable and close to the scripted scene. Then, rehearse the scene again, letting it grow and develop beyond its original ending.

Step 5 – Do It Again
Rehearse the developed scene twice.

Step 6 – Discuss
What did you discover through your rehearsal process? What was challenging about this exercise? What was unexpected? Were you able to stay focused and really listen to your scene partner? Were you able to stay "in the moment", or did you find yourself planning ahead?

This exercise can help you learn to focus on your partner(s), because everyone knows where the scene should go, but no one knows the exact cues, so it is necessary for you to really listen to each other and respond accordingly in order to keep the story going. It can also help you gain a better and more subjective understanding of your character, because you are using your own words to voice your character's needs.

Session Two

Reacting to Your Partner

This session springs out of the previous one. In Session One, we mentioned the importance of focusing and relying on your partner. We will use this session to explore a couple of exercises that might help you establish a deeper understanding of the importance of trusting your partner.

Group Exercise: Trust Fall

This exercise is very popular in acting classes. It's simple, but effective.
Note for the group leader/instructor: for greater safety, you might want to use mats (just in case one actor's weight is too much for the other). Make sure that the actors are evenly paired: you don't want a huge football player paired with a tiny ballerina!

Step 1 – Safety First
Pick a partner. Make sure that your partner has a similar physique.
    Actor A: step in front of your partner.
    Actor B: extend your arms and place your open hands below your partner's shoulders.
    Actor A: slowly lean back, so that your weight gradually rests on B's hands.
    Actor B: You might need to adjust your posture by taking one step back with one leg in order to counterbalance A's weight.
The purpose of this phase is to make sure that B can successfully keep you from falling.

Step 2 – Trust
Once you have established trust, resume the original postures and A, when you are ready, without giving B any warning, allow yourself to fall backwards.

    B: your job is to prevent A from falling; however, wait a split second before catching A, because A needs to experience the sensation of falling, with the fear that entails, in order to better cherish the relief of being caught "in time".

Step 3 – Repeat
Repeat the exercise a couple of times, then switch roles.

Group Exercise: The Blind Walk

This is a quiet exercise: no talking between A and B during the course of the exercise. There will be plenty of time to share thoughts afterwards.

Step 1 – The Bubble
Pick a partner. Make sure that your partner is a similar height.
    Actor A: you will be the leader.
    Actor B: you will be the follower.
(Don't worry! You will get to switch roles!)
    A: place yourself in front of B
    B: extend one of your arms and place your hand on your partner's shoulder. You don't have to hold on to A's shoulder too tightly, but A needs to feel the pressure of your hand.
    A: imagine there is a light, transparent bubble that surrounds both B and you. It's a very fragile bubble. It will break if it bumps into something, and it's important for it to stay intact because it protects both B and you. As the leader, your job is to lead and to protect your follower.

Step 2 – Lead and Follow
Now, the fun part!
    B: close your eyes, and don't cheat!
    A: start walking the space. Remember: make sure you always look for the free space so that the bubble can safely make it through.
Note for the group leader/instructor: during the exercise, side coach by giving the actors instructions such as the following:

    A, start walking slowly, be aware of the entire space, of the positions of the other couples and where they might be going. You can't stop walking, but you can decide to slow down or go faster. Allow some time to establish trust. B has been suddenly deprived of his/her sight: he/she needs time to adjust and to really trust you. You don't want to scare B with sudden movements just yet, but you don't want to make it too easy for him/her. When you think you have established trust, you can start challenging B.
    Start walking at different tempos.
    Explore levels, how close to the floor can you walk? Walk on your tiptoes. Do small jumps. Walk sideways. Backwards. Explore the space. Make sure you don't lose the connection with B, but do not give him/her vocal warnings!

Also, make sure that the Bs don't cheat and open their eyes. You will see that at the beginning partners will be tense and it will take some time for As to establish trust and for Bs to really let go of fear. Then, you will see how incredibly close A and B's movements become. Make sure the actors do not talk during the exercise. Discourage nervous laughter too.

Step 3 – Switch
Continue the exercise for about fifteen minutes, then A should come to a complete stop in a spot in the room that is safe for the bubble. B should open his/her eyes.
Shake it off.
Now switch roles so that A is now in B's position and vice versa and repeat the exercise.

Step 4 – Discuss
Cool off and start a discussion about your experience with the exercise. Was it easier to lead or to follow? Why? Did anyone lose the connection with his or her partner during the exercise? What was that experience like? Did your trust in your partner increase during the exercise?
Variations: B can connect to A by putting the back of his/her hand against the back of A's hand, for example. Or B's forehead to A's palm.

The Blind Walk exercise teaches you about trust and about listening with all of your body. We rely on our eyes so much that we completely forget the potential of the other senses. It might have taken the follower quite some time to adjust, but if the exercise was carried out correctly, the other senses actually began to cover for the loss of sight. The follower got the opportunity to physically understand the importance of trusting his or her partner, while the leader felt the weight of being responsible for someone else's safety.

Go Deeper

Reacting to Your Space

Here, we will explore how much the space, or the environment, can and should influence your performance. We have mentioned this previously, but now we want to focus on it in greater detail.

When you are working in theatre, and particularly in an outdoor venue, space becomes incredibly influential, not just to the performers, but also to the audience. Sometimes the audience can be even more influenced than the actors are. If you are cast in one of the many "Shakespeare in the Park" summer productions, you will likely be on a stage under some powerful lights. If it's July in Louisiana, there is a good chance you will be sweating profusely beneath your costumes. If it's July in Alaska, you might be comfortable, but the audience might feel a little chilly. And of course any outdoor theatre experience wouldn't be complete without the usual idiot passing by who feels the urge to yell something rude. Keep in mind that while it is your job as an actor to "keep going" and endure the challenging climates and conditions, the audience's reaction to these circumstances might be different. They might become noisy; some may even decide to go home.

Audiences can be challenging anywhere, even in an indoor theatre space. We have seen actors using lines to their advantage when responding to external conditions. For example, in a production of *King Lear* in an outdoor summer festival, the actor playing Kent used the line "draw, you whoreson cullionly barber-monger, draw[1]" to shut up someone who had been quite vocal during the performance. Another time, during a performance of *Hamlet*, the actor playing the title role confiscated the cell phone of a man sitting in the front row who had been receiving phone calls and text messages during the performance. Hamlet used the phone as if it were a harmonica for the famous scene with Rosencrantz and Guildenstern. That audience cheered.

Once you are on stage, you take the reins of the show, together with your partners, and reacting to your space becomes a vital part of the performance. But you must keep in mind that your job is to tell the story; the story you have worked so hard to create during rehearsals. If something bothers you, you can acknowledge it in character and go from there. Make sure your choices are appropriate to incorporate into the storytelling and that they do not detract from, or destroy, the world of the play. In the above example, "Stealing" the cell phone from a disrespectful audience didn't harm the story: Hamlet needed a harmonica for that scene (of course he had one in his pocket) and endowing the phone with that identity worked, and at the same time accomplished another goal.

On a different note, the audience can dictate the overall mood of the production. A warm audience inevitably sends positive vibes on stage and the actors will feed off of it and channel that energy back into their performance. On the contrary, a silent audience can suck the energy off of the stage. For comedies in particular, the actors expect the audience to laugh and they respond to that. At times, audiences will laugh at different things than the actors and the director expect them to. Once again,

---

[1] King Lear, Act II, Scene 2 v 33

127

actors must remember the importance of listening! Although you might expect the audience to laugh, it is not a given. If you anticipate it, you might add a beat, and if the audience in doesn't laugh, that beat could turn into an awkward silence, which would break the flow and the pace of the scene.

Everything on stage deserves ongoing attention. You might have rehearsed the scene a million times, but a chair may break, a glass may fall. You have to be able to always react to whatever happens on stage and if you react to your space in the moment you will be able to avoid breaking character if something unexpected happens.

Exercise: Take the Space in and React

This exercise aims at encouraging you to break the habit of walking into a space without taking it in. This is a solo exercise, so please avoid making eye contact with your peers.

Note for the group leader/instructor: Make sure that you have enough time to do this exercise. This exercise can take a long time, and, frankly, it should. In order to break a habit, it takes time! It would be best to do this exercise either on stage or in a big room. You might need to read the questions and instructions aloud to the actors during the exercise. Of course you can add to them, as necessary. Make sure to side coach and remind them to breathe and keep the connection between their breath and their bodies. Side coaching is important because it keeps the actors focused and prevents them from slipping into the "I'm bored" mindset. Observe the actors closely, so you will understand when to move from one step to another.

Step 1 – Walk
Start walking in space.
Touch base with your body. How are you feeling today? As you walk, focus on your feet. Do they hurt? Do they feel alright? Move up to your legs. Are they sore? Do they feel heavy? Continue this screening, concentrating on every part of your body.

Step 2 – Your Breath
Focus on your breath. Visualize the air that you inhale and give it a color. Imagine this air coming into your body and filling every little bit of it. Imagine your body gradually changing color, as the colored air fills it, then exhale and let the color out. As you continue breathing, change the color you give your breath. Does the color choice make any difference? Do you feel any changes in your body as you fill it with air of different colors? What color do you like best?

Step 3 – Balance
Keep walking. Find a rhythm that combines your breath and your pace, so that walking feels easy and natural, as if you could walk for a very long time without feeling tired or bored. As you walk, acknowledge the other people in the room, but think of them as bodies, not as people. How is the space affected by all the bodies in motion? As you walk, attempt to balance the space; the bodies should be evenly distributed in it, as much as possible. If you see a big gap, fill it. Imagine that the space is the main deck of a ship. There is a storm and in order to keep the ship afloat, you have to balance the deck. Does this influence the way you walk? Do you have to adjust the pace? Are you changing your pattern of movement? Continue this balancing act for quite some time, until it becomes natural.

Step 4 – Straight Lines
Now, let's add a feature to your walk: straight lines. Keep walking in the space, balancing it, but walk in straight lines only. If you have to turn, you have to do so on a ninety-degree angle. Continue this for three to five minutes. Does the perception of the space change because of your new way of walking? Are you experiencing the room in a different way? Has your relationship with the other bodies changed?

Step 5 – Curved Lines

Now switch to curves. You have to keep walking, but this time you can only use curves, no straight lines. Do you notice any difference in the way you are experiencing the space? Does it feel better to walk in curves or in straight lines?

Step 6 – Expand

Now forget about balancing the space. As you walk, get as close as possible to one of its limits or borders, like the floor, the walls, the architecture, the door, etc. Don't stop moving. If you are on the floor, crawl, roll, just keep moving. How does the space look from where you are now? Does it feel any different from before?

Step 7 – Clump

Now let's do the opposite: get as close as possible to the other bodies. Clump up. Keep moving, as a group of bodies. Again, how does the perception of the space change as you move in it with this different set of circumstances?

Step 8 – React

Break out of the clump. Walk the space again, balancing it. Choose your own pace. Decide between straight lines or curves, or both. As you walk, allow the space to affect you. If something catches your attention, allow that to surface in your walk. You can change direction, change pace, stop walking, switch from straight lines to curves or vice versa. Allow your entire body to be open to the stimuli coming from the room. Anything can prompt you to react, including the other bodies in the space.

Step 9 – Listen

Extend your attention to sounds. Is there any sound that catches your attention? Is there any noise of traffic coming from outside? Is there any noise in the room? Can you hear the sound of the people walking in the room? Don't force your reactions, but allow yourself to be open to respond. Note for the group leader/instructor: When you see that the actors have achieved a level of awareness of the space that shows engagement with it, let them come to a stop and shake it off. Give them a five minutes break and then let them discuss the experience.

Step 10 – Discuss

Discuss your experiences with this exercise.

Worksheet

Week Ten – Listening

Observe yourself during a face-to-face conversation and take note of your non-verbal responses and reactions to the person or people you are conversing with. Share your observations on the topics below.

My eye contact: _____
_____
_____

My facial expressions: _____
_____
_____

My posture and body language: _____
_____
_____

My non-verbal vocalizations: _____
_____
_____

Now observe someone you consider to be a "good listener" during a face-to-face conversation and take note of his or her non-verbal responses and reactions to the person or people he or she is conversing with. Share your observations on the topics below.

His/her eye contact: _____
_____
_____

His/her facial expressions: _____
_____
_____

His/her posture and body language: _____
_____
_____

His/her non-verbal vocalizations: _____
_____
_____

Week Eleven

Secrets and Surprises

Introduction

You've spent the past ten weeks developing your acting abilities and learning how to bring humanity to the stage. We have further we can go, however, because humans are exceedingly complicated creatures. This week, we will discuss how secrets and surprises can add depth and reality to the portrayal of your characters, layering them with life beyond what can be found in the text.

Secrets

When you approach a character, you have to make the role yours, and you have to figure out the reasons behind your character's behavior. As we have said several times, the script will provide you with information you need, yet imagination and insight are necessary in order to create an organic connection between you and your character's actions. Here's where secrets can be helpful.

What Is a Secret?

You know the answer to that question: a secret is something that someone, for whatever reason, doesn't want to share and/or to make public. The variety of secrets is huge and multifaceted; they can relate to the most personal sphere; they can go way back in the family history. Secrets, if revealed, could be a threat to someone's job, social status and wellbeing. Because of their great power, secrets can dramatically influence our lives in the way we behave and make choices. They could justify the weirdest actions. If you are struggling to understand the reasons behind what your character is doing, you might need to find your character's secret.

Sometimes, secrets are embedded in the scripts. Mind you, we are not looking for secrets that are instrumental to the plot, like the secret marriage in *Romeo and Juliet*, we are looking for something that is not directly related to the development of the story but meaningful for the character's psychological growth. For example, in *Romeo and Juliet*, Juliet's secret could be that she wants to escape from her family because she doesn't want to become like her mother, whose marriage was arranged, like her own is intended to be. This secret doesn't change the love story, but it might give an extra kick to what's at stake for Juliet. As you can see, in this case the secret is built on the given circumstances of the script and on research related to the period in which the story takes place. It is believable that a teenager in Juliet's circumstances could have the ambition of living her own life without the direct intervention of her parents in the matter of love.

A character's secret could also be something not directly related to the story, but related to the character. Iago's secret in *Othello* could be that he was neglected by his parents as a child. This is an example of a secret that is unrelated to the story but related to the character. Or, Iago's secret could be that his marriage with Emilia was arranged and that he has always secretly loved Desdemona. In this case, the secret is related to the story and to the character as well.

Try to determine what your character's secret could be. Is there something that he or she doesn't want to tell, but that is somehow surfacing in his/her actions? The only restriction when looking for your character's secret is that you should always be true to the play. In other words, the secret you settle on cannot be proven wrong by the script.

Secrets allow you to exercise your creativity while building believable fictional scenarios. Because you are the one creating them, you will be able to use them effectively when applying them to your character's actions.

When you find "your secret", you can either keep it to yourself, as part of your own personal character work, or you can share it with the director. It's not advisable to share it with your scene partners, as that might conflict with their own character analysis and work; plus, sharing it with your scene partners could ruin the fun, as it would no longer feels as secretive.

Group Exercise: Open Scene with a Secret

Step 1 – Read
Find a scene partner. Choose an open scene to explore, or your group leader/instructor may assign you a scene. (Open scenes can be found at the end of Week Five.) Working with your scene partner, decide on a situation, characters, and a relationship. Read through the open scene with your partner.

Step 2 – Color the Gray
Make some decisions about your character in order to "color the gray". What is your name? What is your occupation? What is your family situation? Where do you live? How do you feel about the other character(s) in the scene? Etc.

Step 3 – Wants and Ways
Determine what your character wants, and what is keeping him/her from achieving his/her goals. Think of several tactics (both heavy and light) that you might employ in order to succeed. Write them down.

Step 4 – Rehearse
Rehearse the scene a couple of times, making sure you're really listening to your scene partner, taking in your environment, and fighting to achieve your objectives.

Step 5 – Your Secret
Give your character a secret. Make sure it's a secret that makes sense for your character and one that you can buy into. Rehearse the scene again and, if time allows, perform the scene for your group or class.

Step 6 – Discuss
Discuss the exercise with the group. How connected to your character did you feel throughout the process? How successful were you at actively perusing your character's goals? Was it challenging to invent a believable secret for your character? What changed once you gave your character a secret? Did your portrayal of the character change? Did your connection to the character change?

Session Two

Surprises

By the time the lights come up on opening night, you, as the actor, know the play. You've learned your lines, cues, blocking, and business. You know what the other characters will say, if all goes as planned, and you have a pretty good idea of how they will say it. You know how each scene will end (barring an unexpected event) and you know the end of the story. As an actor you know all this, but as a *character* you have no way of knowing how each moment will play out. Your characters have specific expectations, that is, they anticipate particular results from their actions, and because your characters have anticipations and expectations, you have the chance to incorporate the element of surprise into your acting.

Surprises enrich your acting. They necessitate engagement, and they require the intensifying of or modifying of actions. Some surprises are obvious and are required by the text. These surprises are usually on a grander scale. For example, in Tennessee William's *The Glass Menagerie,* Jim kisses Laura and then reveals to her that he is in love with a girl named Betty. This is an example of a surprise required by the text. Laura must be surprised with the revelation in order for the story to be told. Some surprises, however, are created by the work of the actors. These surprises, like secrets, and layers and interest to your acting.

How Do You Create These Surprises?

Surprises are created by anticipating the opposite of what's going to happen. If, in your scene, you know from the script that your lover is going to apologize to your character with his/her next line, you could expect your lover to continue with an argument, or leave, or try to persuade you that he/she is in the right. Because of what you anticipate, your character's defenses are up or your character is furious and ready to attack. When the apology comes, it takes you aback and you must adjust your actions accordingly. This is a surprise that you created for your character. It's not a mouth-open, gasping-in-disbelief, surprise; but it adds depth to your scene and significance to your acting.

Group Exercise: Surprises

Step 1 – Circle
Gather your assigned scene and a pencil. Circle two to three instances in your script where you would like to add the element of surprise for your character. Be creative and make sure you are not choosing obvious, text required surprises.

Step 2 – Rehearse
Get together with your scene partner. Rehearse all the instances that you and your scene partner have chosen (if there are two of you, you should have four to six surprises to work with). Starting a couple lines before, and end a couple lines after, the moment of surprise.

Step 3 – Perform and Discuss
Perform your instances of surprise for the class or group, discussing each moment after performing it.

Go Deeper

Unexpected Gifts

We've discussed the importance of embracing the unexpected and listening so that you are ready to react to what is actually given. In this session, we are going to go deeper by discussing how we should adjust our thinking when it comes to changes, mistakes, and genuine surprises from our scene partners. We will also incorporate secrets and surprises into our second scene showing!

When a mistake happens, we have learned how to use improv to keep the scene moving. In Week Two, we said that you should consider mistakes, "gifts". What did we mean by that? Well, let's look at it this way; as actors we go out of our way to create surprises for our characters. Why? Surprises add depth, realism, excitement, and intensity to our acting. When there is a mistake, a surprise is automatically created, and it's an absolutely genuine surprise, the kind that is impossible for you to create for yourself. In that moment, if you are truly listening, you have the opportunity to react in a completely unplanned fashion, just as the character would.

You might become accustomed to the way your scene partner delivers his lines. Perhaps he does the same thing night after night with little variation. If suddenly one night his inflection changes or he decides to use a completely different strategy, don't be thrown off or break character. Think of it as another gift to you. Mistakes and changes can be your biggest boon if you let them, causing you to focus more intently on your scene partners, and sharpening your purpose.

Next time a mistake happens, rejoice! What an amazing gift! Use it!

Group Exercise: Team Story

Step 1 – Tell a Story
Sit in a circle. One person begins a story with one short sentence. The person to his/her left then takes the story up where he/she left off, adding one short sentence. The story must have a beginning, middle, and end. It's important to not pre-plan. Make sure you accept anything the actor before you says, consider it a gift, and build on it.

Step 2 – Discuss
How successful were you at telling a cohesive story with a beginning, middle, and end? Did you work together well? Were you able to consider what you were given a gift and build on it? Did you get frustrated or confused when what you were given was not what you expected?

Step 3 – Increase the Difficulty
Increase the difficulty by limiting the number of words that each actor can use. You can try three words or less, two words, one word, etc. You can also create hand gestures for punctuation if you like (for instance, slapping the ground could represent a period). Engage in discussion after each storytelling attempt.

Now it's time to put everything we have learned into practice with a scene showing. Remember that this scene showing, like the last, is part of an ongoing process. We continue on the enduring quest to improve and develop the relationship with our characters.

Exercise: Scene Showing

Step 1 – Prepare

Find a quiet place to prepare for your scene showing. You can try reading through some journal entries, listen to music that helps you connect to your character, inhale the scent you chose in the "Scents in Scenes" exercise, or whatever helps you feel connected to your character's emotional state in this moment of the play.

Step 2 – Apply

Perform your scene for the class, applying the skills you've developed through the previous sessions, with a specific emphasis on secrets and surprises. Remember that if something unexpected happens, consider it a gift, and embrace it in character.

Step 3 – Discuss

In which part of your scene did you feel the most connected? Why? Where do you feel you need the most improvement? How did secrets and surprises affect your performance? Did having a secret add depth to your scene? Did creating surprises do anything for your character? Did anything genuinely unexpected happen in your showing? If so, how did you react?

Worksheet

Week Eleven – Secrets and Surprises

Go to a public, typically crowed place, like a park on a sunny Sunday morning, a mall, a gym, a restaurant, or a café. Find a spot where you can sit and observe people, like you did in Week Three. This time, focus on someone who is working. It's important that you don't know him or her. You will need to observe this person for quite some time, so make sure you have a couple of hours at your disposal. Please: don't be creepy! Keep a safe distance and overall, be respectful.

As you observe this person, try to imagine what his/her life is like. Why does he/she work here? Is this his/her dream job? What is his/her family like? Is he/she tired? Is he/she upset? Why? Is he/she pretending to be ok? Why? What does he/she have to lose? Why? Take time to observe this person's physicality, his/her habits, the way he/she is dressed, etc. Do those observations suggest anything to you? If this person is young, is this job a way to pay for college? Please come up with ten to twenty-five other questions about your subject and answer them: the more complete, specific, and accurate your picture of this person is, the better.

In this case, you don't have a script. You don't even know the person you have been observing. This isn't about you finding out the truth. You are not a detective, or a private investigator. You are simply inventing a believable scenario. In order for it to be believable, you have to be consistent with the information that you are generating.

Write your observations, decisions, and answers below:

_____
_____
_____
_____
_____
_____
_____
_____
_____
_____
_____
_____
_____
_____

Now use the information that you have gathered and the backstory you have created to answer the following question:

What is his/her secret? _____

_____

You can repeat the exercise, using a new background story for the person you are observing, and a completely different secret.

Week Twelve

Voice and Body

Introduction

The voice and the body are the tools an actor uses to broadcast the story to the audience. Any obstacle that stands in the way of the audience's ability to see the actions or hear the words is an obstacle that detracts from the success of the play. Don't let that obstacle be you! This week, we will approach voice and body training for the actor.

Note for the group leader/instructor: If your group or class is meeting for longer than fifteen weeks, the following sessions would be a great place to spend a little extra time.

Session One

Voice

Have you ever attended a play where the actors were giving their all, and yet, you couldn't understand a word they said? If you answered "yes", then you will appreciate the importance of vocal training to the actor. Although you could spend years or even decades developing your voice, we will devote this session to studying some vocal basics that are important for every actor to keep in mind.

We can use the acronym C.Y.B.E.R. to help us remember some important basics in our vocal training: Connect Your Breath, Enunciate, and Relax. Let's examine each of these components.

Connect Your Breath

Proper breathing is essential to the actor. Proper breathing supports memorization and focus, and it facilitates **projection**, that is, the ability to fill a space by broadcasting your voice. Proper breath control aids in the removal of tension and the ability to express the widest variety of human emotions. Without proper breath control, your breathing can become shallow and erratic, causing your vocal delivery to suffer. If you cannot control your breathing, you cannot control your voice, and therefore you cannot control the portrayal of your character. You are thus, out-of-control, and the energy you could be spending on listening and pursuing your objectives is instead spent trying to regain control of yourself.

What do we mean by "connect your breath"?

Breathing is an interesting activity. It takes place subconsciously; however, you can also take conscious control of your breathing. When we say "connect your breath", we mean to become consciously aware of the influence of your breathing on every part of your being, and consciously link your breath to what your voice and body are doing.

Let's start with an exercise that aims to strengthen the connection between breath and voice.

Group Exercise: Connect Your Breath, Part 1

Note for the group leader/instructor: You will need to walk the actors through this exercise, reading the instructions and/or questions as needed.

Step 1 – Breathe
Find a place to lie comfortably on the floor. Place a hand on your stomach and feel your breath entering your body and expanding your stomach and then your chest cavity. Why have a hand on your stomach? Because we want you to be sure your breath is *expanding your stomach* when you inhale. Often people don't breathe very deeply and the only thing that expands is their chest cavity.

Step 2 – Fill
Now picture your breath traveling through your body as you inhale. Picture it traveling down your arms into your fingertips. Picture it filling your pelvis, then your legs, all the way down to your toes. Continue to breathe like this for some time.

Step 3 – Connect
Now it's time to connect your breathing to your voice. The next time you exhale, allow sound out with your breath. Don't push the sound out, just allow it to travel out as you exhale, in whatever form it comes. Continue for some time, allowing sound out with every exhale.

Step 4 – Shape
We will now give shape to our connected voice. Try working through the vowel sounds as you exhale. With each exhale, try a different vowel sounds. Then try consonants. Your group leader/instructor can lead you through sounds to try. Make sure you are continuing to breathe deeply, expanding your stomach and chest cavity and visualizing your body filling with air.

Step 5 – Stand and Repeat
Come to your feet and repeat Steps 1 through 4, this time standing. Check your posture, making sure that your shoulders and rib cage are expanded.

Step 6 – Speak
We are going to incorporate language into the exercise. Think of a short line or phrase from your scene. Next time you exhale, let the line or phrase travel out on your breath. Repeat several times, making sure to keep your voice connected to your breath.

Step 7 – Project
Now we're going to add projection to our language. Repeat step 6, but this time as you exhale, try to fill the entire space with your line. It's important to make sure that you are not shouting or tensing up your throat, you are simply filling the space with your voice.

Step 8 – Expand
This time, visualize that you are in a larger area, such as a football stadium. With your next exhale, let the line or phrase travel out on your breath. Again, make sure you are not shouting or tensing your throat and that you are maintaining your breath-voice connection.

Enunciate

Let's take a look at the "E" in our acronym. Enunciation is just as critical to an actor's performance as projection is. The audience needs to hear *and* understand what you are saying in order for the story to be told. Your volume might be loud enough for the little old lady in the back, but without proper enunciation your words might sound like a muddle to her, and, at least for her, the play will be a disappointment and the story won't be told.

One of the simplest (and most fun) ways an actor can work on his or her enunciation is by using tongue twisters. This might seem silly, but it really helps! Frequent work with tongue twisters can help train you to enunciate, and it can also help you connect your thoughts to your voice. Sometimes, in everyday life, our thoughts get ahead of our spoken words and what we want to say comes out jumbled. The same thing can happen, and is more likely to happen, onstage with the added pressure of performance.

Group Exercise: Tongue Twisters

Note for the group leader/instructor: You will need to provide the group or class with several tongue twisters. Alternatively, you can assign that the actors find their own.

Step 1 – Warm-Up

Warm up your mouth, lips, jaw, and entire face. Try making crazy faces at the other actors. Try scrunching your face up as small as possible and then expanding it as much as possible. Try rolling your lips and your tongue.

Step 2 – Rehearse

The group leader or instructor should provide each actor with a tongue twister. Find a space to rehearse your assigned tongue twister. As you are rehearsing your tongue twister, focus on over-enunciating each syllable, concentrating especially on the consonants. (Note: do not over-enunciate the "r" sound onstage. Doing so will affect your lines with an unintended dialect. Obviously, disregard this advice if it is part of a character choice.)

Step 3 – Slowly

Circle up with the group. Choose an actor to begin. The actor should perform his or her tongue twister for the group. The first performance should be very slow and extremely articulate (really go over-the-top with your enunciation!).

Step 4 – Faster

After the first performance, the others in the circle should call out "faster!" and the actor should perform the tongue twister faster, continuing to over-enunciate. Again, the group cries "faster!" and again the actor performs the tongue twister faster. Continue until the actor scrambles the lines, and then move on to the next actor in the circle. The game continues until everyone has had a chance to tackle their tongue twister.

Relax

"R" is the final letter in our acronym and it stands for "relax". We have already discussed the importance of relaxation to the actor, but here we want to emphasize its importance to the actor's vocal performance in particular.

(photo credit: Igor Bulgarin/Shutterstock.com)

Actors have to be able to project their voices, often without the aid of a microphone. They have to ensure that that little old lady at the back of the house can hear every word, while still making their voices sound natural. They might have hours of dialogue, which they have to repeat night after night without exhausting their vocal chords. Sometimes actors have to sing or speak with a challenging dialect. All of this could prove hazardous to the actor's voice if the actor is not relaxed. Tension can cause pain and damage to your vocal chords and it can prevent you from deep breathing, projecting, enunciating, and accessing your full range of emotions. Let's try a very basic relaxation routine to help relax your vocal muscles. Please note that this regimen is in no way all-encompassing, and if you intend to go further in your actor training or vocal training, you will want to work regularly with a professional vocal coach in order to safely improve your vocal performance.

Group Warm-Up: Vocal Relaxation

Step 1 – Breathe

Lie comfortably on the floor like you did in the "Connect Your Breath, Part 1" exercise. Place a hand on your stomach and feel your breath entering your body and expanding your stomach and then your chest cavity.

Step 2 – Fill
Picture your breath traveling through your body as you inhale. Picture it traveling down your arms into your fingertips. Picture it filling your pelvis, then your legs, all the way down to your toes.

Step 3 – Sink
Now, with every exhale, visualize your body sinking into the floor. As you sink into the floor, imagine that tension releases.

Step 4 – Identify Tension and Release
Focus on each part of your body individually, searching for tension. When you identify tension, spend some time in the particular area of your body, imagining the tension releasing into the floor with every exhale.

Step 5 – Face
Direct your focus to your face. With your next inhalation, tighten up the muscles in your face. With your next exhalation, release them. Do this several times.

Step 6 – Face and Neck
Focusing on your face and neck, look for areas of tension and release any tension you discover.

Step 7 – Jaw
Direct your focus to your jaw. Allow your lower jaw to release and fall back towards the floor. Massage the muscles of your cheeks and jaw, concentrating especially on the place where your lower jaw connects below your ears.

Step 8 – Neck
Move to a seated position. Slowly and carefully, tilt your head from side to side. Return to alignment, then gently shake your head as if you're saying no. Carefully alternate between tilting your head from side to side and gently shaking your head as if you you're saying no several times. Remember to return to alignment each time your alternate and be very gentle and careful!

Step 9 – Shoulders
Stand to your feet and roll your shoulders, releasing any tension you are holding in them.

Step 10 – Yawn
Now yawn several times.

Step 11 – Yawn with Sound
Add sound to your yawns. Try using high registers and low registers. Try cycling between the two.

Group Exercise: Connect Your Breath, Part 2

Now that you have completed a simple relaxation warm-up, repeat the "Connect Your Breath, Part 1" exercise and discuss. What changed in the exercise this time around? Did you notice any significant differences that sprung from being more relaxed? What differences did you feel in your body? What differences did you feel in your voice? Did you feel any different emotionally? How could each of the exercises from this session help you as an actor?

Don't stop here! Your voice is an important tool that you use to bring to life all the wonderful, beautiful, sensational words given to you by the playwright. You will want to continue to train and improve it throughout your acting career.

Terms to Remember:
Projection

Session Two

Body

In this session, we will explore ways to awaken the body. As actors, you have to realize that you are your best and only asset; therefore, you have to maximize the use of your instrument. You learned about the voice in the previous session, now it's time to devote some time to the body.

When we watch a live performance, most of its success or failure resides in how much the performers are able to engage us in the action on stage. In order to do so, they are the first ones that have to be engaged!

If you are in a scene on stage, regardless of the number of lines you have to deliver, you need to be present and participate in the storytelling. This could seem challenging if you are playing an ensemble character with little to nothing to do. Yet, if the playwright or director put you in that scene, there is certainly a reason for you to be there. If you are Spear Carrier Number Four in Othello, your reason to be on stage could be to enforce safety, and, as a soldier, you have to be ready to leap into action if necessary. That should be reason enough for you to be engaged and active in the scene.

Beware of posture! As we live our lives, carry ourselves around, we pay little to no attention to posture which oftentimes results in body aches and other painful conditions. As you walk on stage, you immediately capture the attention of the audience. The first few steps you take will leave an impression that might determine how the audience feels about your character. Enter the stage with purpose: there is a reason your character enters, let that reason drive you. Be aware of every part of your body: they all contribute to the purpose of your character and should all be equally engaged.

Your body has a form, and you are lending it to the character. Use the form effectively: it has been proven that a great deal of communication is vehicled by body language. If your character needs to have a specific posture, or has a physical condition, allow your body to embrace it clearly, so that the audience will immediately make the connection and relate it to the character. If no specific posture or condition is necessary, give your character a standard, upright posture and keep it consistent. When you are on stage, you are always seen by the audience: consistency in behavior and posture are a must.

The following exercises are meant to explore the possibilities of body communication to help you understand the importance and the effectiveness of a correct use of the body. First, let's warm up with some walking!

Group Exercise: Walking

Note for the group leader/instructor: In order for actors to have a clear understanding of how to effectively utilize every part of their bodies, they need to be aware of every part of their bodies. This exercise can help them become aware. This exercise should take at least fifteen to twenty minutes, because it takes some time to allow the actors to really commit to it and drop most of their cerebral activity. You can give the instructions and pose the questions provided, adding on, and adjusting to the space you are working in.

Step 1 – Walk

Please walk in the space. At this point, this is a solo exercise, so refrain from making eye contact with your peers or greeting them. As you walk, allow yourself to be open to the space and let it affect you. Is it cold? Is it warm? Is there any particular smell in the air? Do you feel at ease in this space?

Step 2 – Connect

Connect with your breath. As you breathe in, imagine the air flooding into your body and re-vitalizing every single part of it. As you exhale, imagine the air carrying out some of you that becomes part of the space.

Step 3 – Behavioral Patterns

Focus on your behavioral patterns. How fast or slow are you walking? Is this speed in your comfort zone? Do you like walking at this specific speed? Challenge it! Try to walk a little bit faster, or slower. How long can you endure the change? Are you drawn back to the speed in your comfort speed? What is your trajectory? Are you walking in straight lines? Or curves? Are you walking in a loop? Challenge your pattern! If you were walking in straight lines, explore curves. How long can you endure the change?

Step 4 – Imprint

Keep exploring, and as you walk, allow your body to fully participate in this walking. Imagine your body leaving an imprint behind. You want that imprint to be as clear and accurate as possible. Every part of your body should be seen: from your head to your fingers. Does that change the way you are walking? What if the air was thicker? You would have to mold your way through it. Let's try it! Mold your way through this thick air and leave a clear imprint of your path behind. If someone stopped by, he/she should recognize you from the imprint that you left behind, so make sure you are really allowing every part of your body to clearly leave its mark.

Group Exercise:

This exercise is meant to help actors learn how to use their bodies as communication tools. No dialogue should be utilized!

Step 1 – The Scene

Pair up with a partner. Decide who is Person A and who is Person B and read over the scene below.

> Setting: A bare stage with a bench center stage (two chairs will work as well).

> Lights up.
> A enters stage right and sits on the bench.
> Beat.
> B enters stage left and sits on the bench, next to A.
> Beat.
> A stands up and exits stage right.
> B stays on the bench.
> Blackout.

Step 2 – Choices

Now it's time to make choices. Why is A entering the stage? Why is A sitting on the bench? What time is it? Where is this bench? Is it in a park? In a train station? In a waiting room? Somewhere else? Why does A leave? What about B? What is B's motive for entering the stage? How close to A does B want to sit? Why does B stay while A leaves? Do A and B know each other? If so, what is their relationship? What's at stake? What's the conflict?

You have to be very specific and clear and you have to know what you want in order to communicate it. Beware not to mime too much. Your body does not substitute words; it communicates best when using its own language. Sometimes, less is more! Small, clear movements can speak louder than a thousand words. A glance can be extremely effective and tell us a lot about what's going on between you and your partner.

Step 3 – Rehearse and Perform
Once you have made all these decisions, rehearse your scene and perform it for the group or class.

Step 4 – Discuss
Discuss the role of body language in your scene. How effective were you at telling your story through body language?

Step 5 – Repeat
Repeat the exercise, but switch roles with your scene partner.
Variation: The actors can wear neutral masks.

Voice Meet Body

Neither your voice nor your body exists independently. They are both significant parts of your acting instrument. We must learn to unite our instrument into one powerful whole; connecting our voice and body in order to best express the human condition and tell the story. If your body is telling one story and your voice is telling another, your portrayal will fail to be believable and you run the risk of the audience misunderstanding what you are trying to say.

Let's look at an example: An actor is playing the title role in Sophocles' play *Antigone*.

The actor enters the stage with a strong posture, tall and regal. Her body language tells the story of a brave, noble heroine. When she speaks, her voice is weak and crackling. Suddenly, the audience is taken out of the world of the play and is blatantly reminded that the actor is just that, an actor. What they heard didn't match what they saw.

How do you unite your voice and your body in order to best portray characters with real emotions, morals, thoughts, and passions? You can start with a strong foundation, that is, breath. The following exercise will help you use your breathing to connect your voice, body, and emotional state.

Group Exercise: Voice/Body Connection

Step 1 – Stand
Stand facing away from the actors in your group, giving yourself a sense of privacy.

Step 2 – Breathe
Place your hand on your stomach and breathe, feeling your breath expanding your stomach as you inhale. Take a moment to simply breathe.

Step 3 – Contemplate
Choose a bit of text from your assigned scene to work with (just one or two sentences). As you breathe, run the line through your mind. Think about the character's desire behind the line. Picture what is going on in the scene and the reaction your character is getting from the other character(s). Contemplate the stakes for you character at that particular moment in the script. Let the text work on you emotionally.

Step 4 – Your Line
When you feel significantly invested in the line, breathe in, and with your next exhale, deliver the line. Be sure to continue breathing. Breathe as needed during your line delivery.

Step 5 – Emotionally Connect and Move
Repeat the line several times, supporting it with breath. Repeat the line until you feel emotionally connected to the line, and when you do, allow your body to move. Don't feel pressured to make

grand movements or travel the space, but also don't censor yourself. Let your body move as the emotion behind the line inspires it to move.

Step 6 – Repeat and Strengthen
Repeat your line and your movement at least fifteen times, allowing your movement and your vocal choices to change and develop as they connect deeper to the emotions behind your line. Strive for a deeper connection between your vocal and physical choices with each repetition.

Step 7 – Share and Discuss
Share your line with the group and discuss. Did your physical/vocal connection increase with repetition? What role did breath play in facilitating this connection? What discoveries did you make during the course of this exercise?

When discussing the body and voice connection, we should also discuss the scale of physical and vocal choices, that is to say, the size of the physical actions and their vocal components. To unite body and voice, we want to scale these aspects of performance to complement each other. We will now work through an exercise that will illustrate this point, and will help you perform your physical and vocal choices to the same scale.

Group Exercise: 1 through 10

Note for the group leader/instructor: You will need to lead the actors through the exercise, side coaching and reading the instructions aloud when necessary.

Step 1 – Breathe
Spread out in the space and take a moment to connect with your breathing.

Step 2 – No
First, we are going to experience what it feels like when the size of our physical and vocal choices are at odds with each other. Our line for this first part of the exercise is one word; "No". Speak the line.

Step 3 – Speak at 1
We will say that the level at which you spoke this line was a 5 on a scale of 1 to 10. Speak the line again at a 4. Now at a 3. Now at a 2. Finally, speak it at a 1. Repeat it at a 1 several times, taking time to pause, release your breath, and reconnect with your breathing between repetitions. Please note that when we are moving up and down the scale we are adjusting, in effect, the size of the physical and vocal activities, not the intensity. Therefore, a line performed at a "1" can be just as intense as a line performed at a "10" although it won't be as big and loud.

Step 4 – Move at 10
Now we're going to add a physical action to the line. This time when we say "no" at a 1, we will do a physical action at a 10. Trying expanding your arms forcefully, as wide as you can while speaking your line at a 1. Go ahead and try it. Repeat several times, taking note of the incongruity between your voice and your physical action.

Step 5 – Experiment
Take some time to play with your line and your physical action. Try speaking at a 10 and moving at a 1. Try both at a 3, one at a 5 and one at a 1, both at a 10, etc.

Step 6 – Hello Friend
Now, let's move on with a slightly more difficult line. Our new line is "Hello friend." Say the line aloud.

Step 7 – Intention
Think of a backstory and an intention for your line. Once you have come up with these, repeat the line several times, taking time to pause, release your breath, and reconnect with your breathing between repetitions.

Step 8 – Unite
Now invent a physical action that goes with the line. Make sure the movement makes sense with your backstory and intention. Repeat your line along with your physical action several times, attempting to find and feel a clear connection between them in size and intention. With each repetition, let the union between them grow until they are one.

Step 9 – Experiment Again
Now begin playing with the scale of your vocal/physical action. Think of them as one unit now. Your group leader/instructor can coach you up and down the scale.

Step 10 – Discuss
What did it feel like when the size of your movements and voice didn't match? What differences did you notice in your emotional connection once you began to move and speak at the same level? When did you feel most emotionally connected to your body and voice?

Worksheet

Week Twelve – Voice and Movement

What does the acronym C.Y.B.E.R. stand for?: _____
_____

Discuss each part of the acronym and share why you think that part is important for an actor.
C.Y.B. _____
_____
_____
_____
_____

E. _____
_____
_____
_____
_____

R. _____
_____
_____

What did you take away from "Session One: Your Voice"? _____
_____
_____
_____
_____

What did you take away from "Session Two: Your Body"? _____
_____
_____
_____
_____

What did you take away from "Go Deeper: Voice Meet Body"? _____
_____
_____
_____
_____

What was your favorite exercise from this week and why? _____
_____
_____
_____
_____

Week Thirteen

The Director's View

Introduction

This week, we will discuss the director's relationship to the production as well as the actor's relationship to the director. This week's sessions have no exercises included. Instead, we suggest you use your meeting time for discussions on the reading and for in-class scene rehearsal, in order to give actors a taste of what it's like to rehearse with a director.

Session One

The Director's Playground

This session is about working with a director; knowing what to expect and how to relate. Let's start by remembering that theatre is collaborative in its nature, so it is always important for everyone involved in a theatre production to contribute artistically to the process. That being said, it is also important to understand who is responsible for what, and specifically, what the director's role is.

If you remember from Week One, the director is in charge of providing a concept for the production, casting the show, and then working with the actors during rehearsals to bring the script to life on stage. Most directors develop their own aesthetic and have a personal approach to casting, directing, and rehearsing, that's why it's always advisable to research the director you will be working with by trying to attend some of his or her previous productions and by looking at reviews.

(photo credit: Christian Bertrand/Shutterstock.com)

The director's work slightly differs in professional and academic environments. Nonetheless, in both situations, the director is often the charismatic "captain of the ship" who makes sure that everyone is onboard and working towards the same goal. He/she shares his/her vision with the production team, so that a fruitful debate and collaboration can develop. This is also true when it comes to the director's relationship with the actors. The director will have an idea about the world of the play and how to bring it to life, yet, he/she is not going to be on stage: the actors will. For that reason, the actors need to come to rehearsals prepared, not only in terms of memorization, but also in terms of character development and choices. It is critically important that the director and the actors share the same world. In other words: the director provides the sandbox in which actors get to play. There are an infinite array of possibilities regarding what the actors can do within the sandbox, but they should not get out of the sandbox.

In the professional world, sometimes the director isn't completely in charge of casting: a casting director will go to general auditions and only call a few actors back for the director to see. At times, the producer directly hires some actors. That is the case, for example, in some Broadway productions featuring famous guest stars. But the director normally has the final word on casting, and the producers will usually attempt to comply with his/her artistic vision. If you are working on a professional production, the director will expect you to "do your work" outside of rehearsals. It's not unusual for professional directors to require actors to be off book on the first day of rehearsals, for example. The director will be there to discuss your choices, but he/she will be eager to see what you bring to the table.

As far as blocking is concerned, some directors are very dictatorial about stage movement, others are not at all. It is, ultimately, the job of the director to make sure that sightlines are clear and that actors don't get upstaged by other actors or by the set. Blocking adjustments are to be expected throughout the rehearsal process. Just remember, when it comes to blocking, the most important thing is to make sure that your movements are justified. If you feel the urgency to move, then do it. If a director tells you to cross downstage left on cue, it might be because he/she sees a shift in the character that requires a change in the staging. Try to think of what that could be and you will be able to motivate the blocking rather than just simply executing it.

Directors will also provide the actors – through the stage manager – a detailed rehearsal schedule, so that actors will know when they are called, and for how long. In the professional world, where actors and productions are supervised by the **Actors' Equity Association** (the American labor union that represents actors and stage managers), it's imperative to be efficient when it comes to rehearsal time. Time is money after all, and that is true for all professional productions. Actors should not be called to hang out in the theatre or in the green room doing nothing. Conversely, if actors don't show up at their call time, they might face big trouble, and ultimately, be fired. So watch out!

Actors' Equity Association also establishes that the directors should complete their work with the actors by tech week. In other words, the actors should be left alone with what they have collaboratively created during the rehearsal process while the heavy technical elements are introduced to the production, right before opening night. No additional acting directions should be given and the stage manager is in charge of enforcing this rule. The rationale behind this is that for a number of days, weeks, or months, the actors and the director have been devoting most of their time to focusing on and developing moments, motives, themes, etc. When tech week begins, actors get overwhelmed by the bombardment of external technical stimuli that can require them to make adjustments.

In academia, the role of the director in a production might be a little more comprehensive. In some programs, theatre productions are actual classes; therefore, the director is also the instructor, with all that that entails, grading included. Academic theatre is more process oriented than product oriented, so even if a successful opening night is the end goal, the director's role mostly entails helping student actors find their own voices within their characters throughout the rehearsal process. Normally, colleges and universities have longer rehearsal processes and can take advantage of their own performance facilities the entire time, which is almost never the case with professional productions. Longer rehearsal processes mean more commitment from students and from faculty, including the director. Despite the different environment, the director will require the same professional demeanor from student actors. The actors will still be expected to come to rehearsals on time and to work on their character on their own in order to bring ideas to the table. The director will be there to help student actors and to teach. To some extent, he/she can be considered a mentor, that is to say someone who provides technical advice on the art and craft of the stage and who is ultimately interested in the academic growth of the student in order to prepare him or her for the professional world. Don't assume that an academic production is less serious or less important than a professional one, though. Your director will expect you to be on time, prepared and willing to learn and if you do not comply, you will be recast and/or receive a failing grade.

Terms to Remember:

Actors' Equity Association

Your Playground

When you are cast in a role, the director will become the person you will relate to the most in terms of artistic choices and decisions about your character. As previously stated, the director will provide you the general concept for the show, and the world in which all the characters should live, but that doesn't mean you will be deprived of the freedom to build your own character.

As you begin your journey in a role, the script becomes your playground. That is where you will be able to acquire information about your character. The more data and gold nuggets you find, the more specific your choices will be and the richer your discussion will be with the director. It is important that you write down all that happens to your character: everything significant that you can gather from the moment he/she was born. Basically, you should uncover and create your character's biography.

Professional actors tend to be very meticulous in looking for this information and they often write it down in the form of a timeline. The timeline is the visual representation of the life of your character. It starts with his or her birth and then moves on. Every fact or event that happens in his/her life becomes a point in the line, up until the end of the play. Actors try to make the timeline as detailed as possible; therefore, the line can become very long and extremely packed with points. This detail helps with understanding and visualizing all that your character has gone through and everything that might influence his/her behavior. Other actors prefer to list everything in their character journal rather than marking it down on a line. Either way is fine, really, but the important thing is collecting information. The more information you collect, the more accurate your performance. The director will not ask you to see your timeline or your list, but it will be part of your personal research.

Other elements of research will depend on the nature of your role. For example, if you are cast in a Shakespeare play, the interpreting, the scansion, and all the language work will be part of your job. Similarly, if the character you are playing has a specific physical or psychological condition, you should research its symptoms and observe how they manifest themselves. For example, Eddie Redmayne revealed in an interview that he visited several hospitals where he observed and interacted with patients with ALS while he was working on his Academy Award winning performance of Stephen Hawking in *The Theory of Everything*. The character's world, his/her humanity, and his/her physical condition are entirely your domain. The director will rarely do the research for you. He/she will expect you to do it for yourself.

Finally, let's introduce rehearsal etiquette. Below you will find an example of some the etiquette "rules" that will be enforced by the stage manager, following the director's instructions. Most of these rules are common sense, and their goal is to facilitate the rehearsal process and avoid unwanted conflicts or drama off stage.

1. Show up on time and ready to work.
2. Know your lines.
3. Do your homework and research on the role, and bring ideas to the table.
4. Eliminate outside distractions. Turn off cell phones.

5. Leave personal problems at home.
6. Respect the physical space: don't leave your stuff behind when rehearsal is over.
7. Be hygienic and stay clean.
8. Be respectful about touch.
9. Stay focused during rehearsals. Be aware of the space, of your conditions, and of the others' conditions.
10. Wear comfortable, appropriate clothing and shoes. Don't rehearse barefoot.
11. Respect the many collaborators.
12. Don't play with props and check your props. (Note that sometimes glass is banned from stage for safety reasons.)
13. Listen and be open to new ideas. Remain fully present and receptive to direction.
14. Pay attention and don't get the same note twice. Write your notes down if you need to.
15. Be worthy of trust. Don't gossip.
16. Be childlike but never childish. Act with creative impulse but never with thoughtlessness.
17. Set high standards for yourself.
18. Communicate your conflicts in a timely fashion.
19. Inspire others with your example.

This is just an example; directors might come up with other rules that are more specific to the production. As mentioned, the stage manager will enforce the rules and will take the task seriously (for instance, being late to rehearsal may result in your replacement).

Go Deeper

Respect the Playwright!

This session is just a friendly reminder of how important it is to respect everyone's work, starting with the work of the playwright.

The playwright has a story that he or she wants to share, and it is your responsibility to honor that story. It is imperative that you give your greatest effort to memorizing the lines as they are written, without paraphrasing. The playwright chose those specific words for a reason. If the lines don't make sense to you, read them over and over again and try to determine the logic of the language. If your character uses language that you don't particularly care for, you have two choices. You can either find a way to embrace it, realizing that it is part of what makes your character who he/she is, or you can choose not to audition for the role in the first place. Changing the language can get yourself and the production into big trouble. Most plays are covered by copyright law, and if the production doesn't respect the restrictions imposed by the law, the playwright and/or the publishers might shut down the production.

For plays that are in the public domain, it's a little different. As you probably know, if the playwright has been dead for over seventy years, the play is likely in the public domain. Plays in the public domain do not require royalties to produce. Molière's plays are in the public domain if performed in the original French, but if you are using a translation, you will need to check its date, as you might have to pay royalties to the translator. Shakespeare's plays are clearly in the public domain if performed in their original language. And, if you think that you can paraphrase Shakespeare and do a better job, please consider a career as a playwright instead of as an actor!

Worksheet

Week Thirteen – The Director's View

Have you experienced working with a director in a past production? _____

If so, give some specific examples of how the director contributed to the success of the production. If you haven't experience working with a director, give some examples of specific ways you believe a director could contribute to your scene work: _____
_____
_____
_____
_____
_____
_____
_____
_____
_____
_____

From your own experiences, or in own opinion, what are some of the challenges actors face when working with a director? _____
_____
_____
_____
_____
_____
_____
_____
_____
_____
_____
_____

What are some ways that actors could have, or can, overcome those challenges? _____
_____
_____
_____
_____
_____
_____
_____
_____
_____

Week Fourteen

Monologues

Introduction

This week is all about monologues and how you prepare them for an audition. Monologues can be intimidating, but with the proper tools and a positive attitude, you can truly have fun crafting active pieces to be proud of!

Session One

What Is a Monologue?

First of all, what is a **monologue**? According to the Oxford Dictionary, a monologue is: "A long speech given by an actor in a play or film, or as part of a theatrical or broadcast programme." According to the same dictionary, a monologue is also: "A long, tedious speech given by one person during a conversation."

This is a very good place to start. Let's analyze this definition.

A monologue is said to be "a long speech". Yes, but how long? Well, most actors will tell you that a one-minute monologue can feel awfully long. Yet, there are one-man shows that last over one hour. . . . How is that for a long monologue! Usually, good auditioning monologues span between forty-five seconds and two minutes, but in plays, they could be much, much longer. The longer the monologue, the greater the challenge for the actor, and not really because of memorization, but rather because of the need to keep it active (more about this later).

In a monologue, a character often "speaks his or her mind" about something that is important enough to deserve some extra words. When dialogue alone can't justify or make sense of the character's actions, the character needs to clarify. We do this in real life, more frequently than we think. The difference is that in real life we have no problem ranting for minutes about something, while on stage, playwrights need to make sure that the character doesn't go on forever pointlessly. A monologue, to be effective, needs to make a point, or explore an issue, with the least amount of words possible.

Usually, monologues "happen" in the middle of the dialogue between two or more characters. This is very important! Monologues are intended to be directed towards a partner! Nowadays, you can find several collections of monologues gathered in monologue books, or look online and an overwhelming amount of options will pop up. But be careful! A monologue, regardless of how good it is, is functional to a specific character in a specific play. Although you might just be using it for an audition where only a one- to two-minute monologue is required, you want to know as much as possible about the character and the play the monologue is from. And you have to know to whom you are addressing it: who would your partner onstage be, if you were playing the role in the scene?

(photo credit: MANDY GODBEHEAR/Shutterstock.com)

It is very important to play the monologue as if you were addressing your partner, because otherwise you will come across as someone who has memorized some lines and now is randomly delivering them. As we have mentioned before, a monologue needs to prove a point. Think about it: if you want to prove a point, you want to prove it to someone! If you need to convince someone of something, you will have an objective and you will use actions/tactics/strategies along with your lines. That's why the "invisible" partner, in an audition, is so important: if you don't have one, your mind will disengage and you will stop playing actions.

You will hear about dramatic, comedic, contemporary, and period/classic monologues.

A dramatic monologue is usually emotionally charged and has the character fighting for something he/she really cares about. Dramatic monologues cover serious topics. Conversely, comedic monologues go for the laugh. They are usually fast paced and rely a lot on the actor's abilities of physicalization.

Monologues taken out of contemporary plays are, obviously, contemporary. Of course, you can have contemporary dramatic and contemporary comedic monologues. The distinguishing feature of these monologues is that the language is close to what we speak here and now.

Classic or period monologues come from classic or period plays, such as plays written by Shakespeare, Molière, or Chekhov. They could be either dramatic or comedic and they usually challenge the actor because of the language and the style.

You have probably heard the word **soliloquy**. Is it the same as a monologue? No, it's a different situation. If a character is on stage alone during his/her speech, it is a soliloquy. For example, Hamlet's "To be, or not to be" speech is a soliloquy, not a monologue, because he is alone in the crypt. Soliloquies are even more challenging for the actor because the character is actually speaking to himself/herself. In order to make them active, the actor needs to really focus on why he or she is speaking those particular words and discover/create an imaginary/psychological partner. Are the words possibly intended to be heard by God? By Society? By Yorick (think of the above mentioned Hamlet's soliloquy)? Is the character speaking to a part of himself/herself in order to convince himself/herself of something and achieve a goal? This is a decision that the actor – together with the director – has to make in order to keep the action moving.

At the beginning of this section, I called one-person shows long monologues. Is that correct or should they be called soliloquies, since the actor is alone on stage? Although generalizing isn't always appropriate, it's safe to say that one-person shows are monologues because the actor, in one way or another, is breaking the fourth wall, that is, speaking directly to the audience. The character is telling his/her story to someone, and the actor playing the role identifies that someone with the audience.

Group Exercise: Team Monologue

Note: This exercise is a variation/composite of the "Team Story" exercise that can be found in Week Eleven and the "Strategy Switch-Up" exercise from Week Nine.

Step 1 – Decide
Sit in a circle. Together as a group, decide on a character, a situation, and a location. Agree on who the character is talking to and what the character wants from the other character.

Step 2 – Write
As a group, think of seven or more strategies/actions/tactics and write each one on a piece of paper.

Step 3 – Sort
Divide your tactics into two piles: heavy tactics and light tactics.

Step 4 – The Monologue
The leader should draw a tactic sign from one of the piles and hold it up. The first actor should begin the monologue with one short sentence, using the tactic to try and achieve the character's goal. The actor to his/her left then takes up the monologue where the first actor left off, adding one short sentence. Throughout the monologue, whenever the group leader sees fit, he/she can hold up a new tactic sign, alternating between light and heavy tactics.

Note: Be sure to speak the monologue from the character's point of view, staying in character and accepting and building on anything the actor before you gives you.

Step 5 – Increase the Difficulty
Try another monologue, with a different character, situation, location, and goal. You can use the same tactic signs (shuffling them) or create new ones. Increase the difficulty by limiting the number of words that each actor can use. You can try three words or less, two words, one word, etc. You can also create hand gestures for punctuation if you like (for instance, slapping the ground could represent a period). Engage in discussion after each monologue.

Group Exercise:

Note for the group leader/instructor: For this exercise, and for exercises in future sessions, each actor will need to have an appropriate monologue to work with. It's recommended that you provide monologues for the actors. Alternatively, you can assign that the actors find their own monologues.

Step 1 – Read
Read over your assigned monologue on your own, then read it aloud to the group.

Step 2 – Research, Invent, and Discuss
Who is your character talking to and what is your character's relationship with him/her? What is your character's background? What does your character want? How might he/she go about getting it?

Terms to Remember:

Monologue   Soliloquy

More than Words

Let's spend some time analyzing a monologue.

The following is a monologue from Oscar Wilde's play *Lady Windermere's Fan*[1]. In the play, Lady Windermere suspects that her husband is having an affair with Mrs. Erlynne, but he denies it. When the suspected lover shows up at her birthday party, invited by her husband, Lady Windermere resolves to leave him and run away with a lover of her own. Throughout the play some painful truths are uncovered. It is revealed that Mrs. Erlynne is Lady Windermere's long lost mother, who left Lady Windermere's father and abandoned her child for a lover, only to later be abandoned herself to a life of shame and misery. When Mrs. Erlynne confronts Lady Windermere in order to persuade her to return to her husband, Lady Windermere does not know who Mrs. Erlynne really is; she still assumes that Mrs. Erlynne is her husband's lover.

What you will read below is the final part of the long monologue that Mrs. Erlynne uses in an attempt to stop Lady Windermere from making the same mistake she made.

MRS. ERLYNNE
Go back, Lady Windermere, to the husband who loves you, whom you love. You have a child, Lady Windermere. Go back to that child who even now, in pain or in joy, may be calling to you. God gave you that child. He will require from you that you make his life fine, that you watch over him. What answer will you make to God if his life is ruined through you? Back to your house, Lady Windermere – your husband loves you! He has never swerved for a moment from the love he bears you. But even if he had a thousand loves, you must stay with your child. If he was harsh to you, you must stay with your child. If he ill-treated you, you must stay with your child. If he abandoned you, your place is with your child.

As you can see, this monologue is very straightforward. Mrs. Erlynne is directly addressing Lady Windermere. Therefore, it would be advisable that the actor performing this monologue for an audition create an imaginary partner in the house and address the monologue to this partner.

Look at the sentences: they are all short and precise. From the very beginning, they are mostly orders. "Go back", or just "back" is said three times. Why? Because that is Mrs. Erlynne's main objective: she wants Lady Windermere not to leave her husband and child. What actions is she playing? The structure of the monologue suggests that she is firmly ordering her to reconsider her decision. She is summoning God as the ultimate threat: "God gave you a child. He will require from you that you make his life fine, that you watch over him. What answer will you make to God if his life is ruined through you?"

It's important to note that in the play, as we mentioned, this is the ending of a longer monologue and that Lady Windermere is being addressed. It is taking Mrs. Erlynne a long time to persuade Lady

---

[1] Lady Windermere's Fan. Oscar Wilde. London, Elkin Mathews, 1893

Windermere, who is resisting. This is crucial, and this is also why this is a good monologue: Mrs. Erlynne needs to "fight" for the whole duration of her speech in order to win Lady Windermere over.

Why would Lady Windermere listen to her? She doesn't know Mrs. Erlynne is her mother, she was told her mother had died. So here is this woman confronting her, hinting at the depths of her own tragedy and disgrace, and speaking about what lengths she had to go to survive. This is a lot for anyone to take in all at once, so that's why the full monologue is quite long. It takes time for Lady Windermere to receive all of this and to resolve to act. Please take a look below at the whole monologue.

MRS. ERLYNNE
Believe what you choose about me. I am not worth a moment's sorrow. But don't spoil your beautiful young life on my account! You don't know what may be in store for you, unless you leave this house at once. You don't know what it is to fall into the pit, to be despised, mocked, abandoned, sneered at – to be an outcast! to find the door shut against one, to have to creep in by hideous byways, afraid every moment lest the mask should be stripped from one's face, and all the while to hear the laughter, the horrible laughter of the world, a thing more tragic than all the tears the world has ever shed. You don't know what it is. One pays for one's sins, and then one pays again, and all one's life one pays. You must never know that. – As for me, if suffering be an expiation, then at this moment I have expiated all my faults, whatever they have been; for tonight you have made a heart in one who had it not, made it and broken it. – But let that pass. I may have wrecked my own life, but I will not let you wreck yours. You – why, you are a mere girl, you would be lost. You haven't got the kind of brains that enables a woman to get back. You have neither the wit nor the courage. You couldn't stand dishonor! No! Go back, Lady Windermere, to the husband who loves you, whom you love. You have a child, Lady Windermere. Go back to that child who even now, in pain or in joy, may be calling to you. God gave you that child. He will require from you that you make his life fine, that you watch over him. What answer will you make to God if his life is ruined through you? Back to your house, Lady Windermere – your husband loves you! He has never swerved for a moment from the love he bears you. But even if he had a thousand loves, you must stay with your child. If he was harsh to you, you must stay with your child. If he ill-treated you, you must stay with your child. If he abandoned you, your place is with your child.

If you are performing this monologue for an audition, quite likely you will only use the cut starting with "Go back". That will give you enough material to really make your point. Yet, to best utilize the monologue, you should be acquainted with the whole play and with the character that you are playing. Sometimes, directors or casting agents might want to test the actors about their process, and they might ask "have you read the play?" or "what's at stake for Mrs. Erlynne now?", or "what does she have to loose?". Unless you have read the play and done your character work, you won't be able to provide a satisfactory answer, and believe us, it will show. In particular, if your monologue, like this one, comes from a well-known play, the director will more than likely be familiar with it.

Let's talk about action for a minute.

If you are performing a monologue, you are probably auditioning. Let's assume that you are using the shorter, cut version of Mrs. Erlynne's monologue. As we have said, she is confronting Lady Windermere. You, playing Mrs. Erlynne, *want* Lady Windermere to go back to her family, and you order (that is your *action*) her to stay. When you pick an action, make sure that it is strong, exciting, and relates directly to the other character onstage. For example, Mrs. Erlynne could "talk Lady Windermere through her decision" instead, but that would result in a much weaker performance. Also, try adding variety to your monologue by playing more that one tactic/action/strategy. Mrs. Erlynne's goal/want could be to get her daughter to return home, and she uses the action "to order", but can you find places within the monologue where she can use different actions? "To order" is a fairly heavy action, and from our analysis, we would probably deduce that most of Mrs. Erlynne's tactics in this monologue would be heavy, but can you find a place where she might use a lighter strategy? Why do we need this variety? First, it keeps the audience engaged, and second, it shows the director or casting agent that you can be flexible.

It is also important to remember that every time a particular action fails, Mrs. Erlynne needs to fight harder, which suggests that she really cares. That is actually the key: because she cares, her stakes have to be high! She doesn't want her daughter to end up like herself, disgraced and pitiful. If you identify with her, you will feel the need to overcome the obstacle – Lady Windermere's resistance to resolving to stay with her family – and to really use each line as yet another attempt at hitting the target and ultimately, winning.

In terms of physicality, make sure you stay true to yourself, and to the character. If you feel like you should move, then move. But if you feel like you should hold your ground, then do that. You don't have to showcase your abilities to walk around and perform crazy physical stunts: you have to show your ability to convey a strong message in a short amount of time.

Remember that imaginary scene partner that we mentioned? The following exercise will help you learn to work with that imaginary other.

Group Exercise: Invisible Scene Partner

Step 1 – Read and Describe
Find a partner. Partner A will read his or her monologue to Partner B. Partner A should explain the situation in which the monologue takes place and describe the character that he/she is talking to and the relationship between characters.

Step 2 – Deliver and React
Partner A will now deliver the monologue to Partner B, while Partner B plays the other character in the scene. It is important that B reacts to what A is giving, just as the character would. Partner A should note the reactions from B.

Step 3 – Change it Up
Do it again, and this time Partner B should react differently to what Partner A is giving.

Step 4 – Discuss
Discuss the reactions A got from B. Discuss which reactions especially helped A fight harder in pursuit of his/her goal.

Step 5 – Mark
Partner A should take a moment to mark three to five specific places in the monologue that he/she will imagine specific reactions from the other character in the scene.

Step 6 – Perform
Now Partner A should perform the monologue to an imaginary "other". Partner B can watch, but Partner A should pick a specific, empty place in front of him or her and place his/her imaginary scene partner there.

Step 7 – Repeat
Repeat the exercise, this time focusing on Partner B's monologue.

It's important to note that when you are performing a monologue for a director or casting agent, you can remain open to them by placing your imaginary scene partner near them; however, do not deliver the monologue directly to them. Delivering the monologue directly to the director/casting agent could make them uncomfortable, as they could feel pressured to "act" in the scene with you and that could distract them from evaluating your amazing performance!

Exercise: Monologue Analysis

Find a quiet place and analyze your assigned monologue, applying all the tools you've learned to apply to your scenes. When you are finished, share your analysis with your group or class.

Go Deeper

Pick the Right One!

Selecting a monologue for an audition can be one of the most excruciating tasks for an actor. Unfortunately, it's quite unlikely that this session will give you the perfect strategy to find your perfect monologue, but it might give you some ideas about what to look for and what to avoid.

As directors, we have sat through many auditions and have heard countless monologues. Sometimes, as we hear the first word of a monologue, we automatically think "Oh, no. . . .". In this session, we have included some of the things that make us think that.

If you've selected a classic monologue, or something that is in the public domain, more than likely the director will be familiar with it. This is not necessarily a bad thing, but the director might have expectations about it. Again, nothing necessarily bad about that, but it is something to be aware of and take into consideration. What we would strongly suggest you not do though, is to pick a classic monologue that is very far from your age range. If you are a teenager, please look for monologues within your age range. Although in high schools and colleges classic plays are a frequent production choice and all characters will be played by very young adults, during the audition, it is still preferable to pick something that best showcases where you are now, rather than were you will be in say, thirty years.

(photo credit: Julia Kaysa/ Shutterstock.com)

Here is an example from Kiara Pipino:

"In a professional audition, I saw a seventeen-year-old girl performing the "Out, damned spot" monologue from *Macbeth*. That was one of my "Oh no . . ." moments. She did a fine job with the language, she showed she knew what she was saying – which is one of the challenges in Shakespeare – but she looked like more of an Ophelia to me. Interestingly, Lady Macbeth and Ophelia share the same trait at some point: madness, so I guess my reaction was hindered by the knowledge of the play rather than from the abilities of the actress. If I had been able to suggest a monologue for her, I would have probably told her to look at Ophelia's."

This leads us to another tip about classic monologues. You have to make sure you know the meaning of every word that you are saying. Shakespeare wrote his plays mostly in iambic pentameter some four hundred years ago. It is no surprise we don't talk like that anymore! The first thing you should do when working with one of his monologues is to go ahead and rewrite it in your own words, researching the meaning behind any words or phrases that you don't understand. You, of course, won't perform it in your own words, but the exercise will help you personalize and comprehend what you are saying. In a production, if you thoroughly understand everything you say, the audience will also understand it. Remember that you had time to learn the piece, but the audience didn't, and there is a good chance that this is the very first time they are hearing this speech. If you are auditioning, the director might know the language very well, but he/she will still be interested in seeing if you do.

This is approach is true for all classic and period style pieces, from Greek Theatre to Chekhov. If you are selecting a classic monologue that wasn't originally written in English, do yourself a favor and find and compare different translations. Sophocles' plays, for instance, have been translated a million times, so look for the translation that suits you (or the audition) the best. If you are auditioning for a production of, let's say, *Antigone*, you will probably be asked to bring a classic monologue. Sometimes, directors prefer to hear monologues from a play other than the one they are casting, and sometimes that's not the case. You will get this information from the casting call. Regardless, you will want to know which translation the director intends to use, because that will give you a hint about the kind of language that the production intends to pursue and you'll have the opportunity to look for a monologue from another Greek play with the same translator.

Another "Oh no . . ." moment: when actors pick a classic Greek monologue with an early 20th century translation, because it was the first result that popped up in their internet search. Unless specifically required by the production, please don't choose super early translations.

Moving on. You want your monologue to be active, and to give you the opportunity to do something special with it in order to show the casting director what you can do. Yet, you don't want it to be "too much" or "overacted". Think about it and do your research. Who are you auditioning for? That's a very important question that has a lot to do with the piece you are picking. Knowing your audience is part of the deal. You don't want to offend anybody, if you want the job, that is. For example, if you are auditioning for a children's theatre, there is no need to pick a piece with a lot of foul language.

You will always hear acting teachers telling you to "make bold choices" and that is true, most of the times. In an audition, you want to make choices, but you have to make sure that those choices stay true to the action within the monologue. In other words, don't make "bold choices" just for the heck of making bold choices. For example, in Mrs. Erlynne's monologue, there would be no need to, say, throw a chair on the floor just to show the casting director that you can have an outburst of rage while delivering a monologue. As bold as throwing a chair on the floor might be, is it really consistent with the character?

If you can, avoid picking monologues from very well-known plays, and that is true for both classic and contemporary pieces. Everyone has an idea about the "To be, or not to be" monologue, and you don't have the time in an audition to challenge the director's idea and win him/her over.

Another "Oh no . . ." moment: when an actor is auditioning for a theatre production with a monologue from a movie. Don't do that. Just don't. And don't use a song as a monologue. Once a student actor auditioned with a Bob Dylan song that he had turned into a monologue. Great song, but it didn't work as a dramatic monologue. Songs are usually not conceived to be very active. They do have a message or make a point, but they shy away from conflict, which is ultimately what is theatrically successful.

It's not advisable to pick monologues from plays that are currently playing on Broadway, in the theatre next door, that have been previously directed by the person you are auditioning for, or that have been produced recently by the theatre/college that you are auditioning for. Everyone will have an opinion about those monologues, you included. Again, you don't have the time to prove anyone wrong in a two-minute audition.

This might sound banal, but look for a monologue that showcases your strengths. If you get cast, you will have plenty of time to prove to the director that you are versatile and can even play against your strengths. Just get the role first.

Sometimes, you will be asked to prepare two contrasting monologues. This means you are required to bring two monologues that showcase two opposite features. Unless the casting call specifies it differently, that usually means that you have to pick a dramatic monologue and a comedic one. Period pieces are at times considered contrasting with contemporary ones, but you might want to make sure before picking a monologue from Arthur Miller's *The Crucible* and Euripides' *Medea*.

When you have to audition with contrasting monologues, the toughest part is the transition between the two pieces. You want the two moments to be distinct, but you don't want a blackout because you don't want to loose the energy of the moment. The challenge therefore becomes picking two pieces that, despite the contrast, could play some of the same "chords" so that you can use one of those chords as the pivot from the first piece into the second.

One last word about dramatic monologues. It's true that showing the ability to access a wide variety of emotions is key in an actor, but it's also true that showing a hundred different emotions in a one-minute monologue is utterly impossible. If a character is brought to tears, it usually happens as a result of a series of events in a scene and the monologue might be the climactic moment of that scene. If you are cast in that role, you will be helped by your character's journey in the scene so that by the time you reach that monologue, the tears will come organically, rather than artificially. It's very hard to reproduce that organic reaction in an audition and even if you might have the ability to "cry on cue" (we have read that many times on résumés), you want to make sure that you stay truthful to the moment rather than emoting for the sake of a tear.

Finally, and this is probably the most important piece of advice regarding monologue selection, you should pick a monologue that you like, one that you have fun exploring. You need to find an affinity with it, and something that will keep you wondering about it. Eventually, if you want to be a professional actor, you will have to memorize lots and lots of lines and lots and lots of monologues. You want to build a repertoire of monologues that you can use for any audition. Most professional actors have anywhere between twenty and thirty monologues memorized and ready to go at any time. So, when you choose one, you really need to like it, so that it will stay with you and will be easy to refresh, regardless of the number of monologues that you do.

Group Discussion: Your Monologue

Look over your assigned/chosen monologue and decide whether or not you think it would be a good monologue to use in an audition. Discuss your conclusion with the group. What features of the monologue are desirable for an audition? What features of the monologue are not ideal for an audition?

Group Exercise: Monologue Performance

Step 1 – Perform
Perform your assigned/chosen monologue for the group or class as if you were performing it an audition.

Step 2 – Discuss
What worked in your performance? What didn't work so well? If you were to do this monologue in an actual audition, what would you do differently?

Step 3 – Repeat
If time allows, perform the monologue a second time, making appropriate adjustments and improvements.

Worksheet

Week Fourteen – Monologues

Take a look at the script that your assigned monologue is taken from. Look for clues in the script about what your character likes, his or her activities, relationships, values, and anything else you can find and then fill out the information below from your character's point of view. Invent any information that is not provided for you in the script, but be sure it stays true to the world of the play.

Name: _____

Do you have a nickname? What is it and how did you get it?: _____

What is your age and how old do you feel?: _____

What is your social and economic status: _____

What is your favorite color and why?: _____

What is your favorite type of music and why?: _____

What is your favorite food and why?: _____

What is a favorite memory you have and why?: _____

_____

Who do you consider to be your closest friends?: _____

_____

Who do you consider enemies and why?: _____

_____

Who are your family members?: _____

_____

How close are you to your family members and how do you feel about them?: _____

_____

How do you feel about the character(s) that you are speaking your monologue to?: _____

_____

_____

How do you think that that/those character(s) feel(s) about you?: _____

_____

Why? _____

_____

Do you consider yourself an introvert or an extrovert?: _____

Do others consider you an introvert or an extrovert?: _____

Do you consider yourself a leader or a follower?: _____

Do others consider you a leader or a follower?: _____

What animal are you most like and why?: _____

_____

What five adjectives best describe you?: _____

During your monologue, what is your objective? (What do you want from the other character or characters onstage?) _____

_____

Why do you want that? _____

_____

Week Fifteen

Auditioning

Introduction

This information logically follows what you learned in Week Fourteen about monologues. As a matter of fact, you have read a great deal about what to do during auditions already. This week, we would like to focus on some specific elements of your audition.

Session One

Etiquette

Regardless of if you are auditioning for a professional production, for an undergraduate or graduate theatre program or for a community theatre, the very first thing that you have to do is to research the people you will be auditioning for, the theatre or the theatre program, and the play/plays they are casting. This is mandatory for several reasons. First, you need to make sure that you actually want to audition for them. Sometimes, actors try to audition as much as possible and they don't even bother spending any time in this pre-audition research. Sure, auditioning as much as possible is great; it increases your visibility, introduces you to people, gives you a chance to test your monologues, and builds your confidence. Yet you don't want to put yourself in the situation of upsetting a director by turning down a role.

Kiara recalls her personal experience with this:

"Years ago, I was part of a professional production of *Hair*. Hundreds of actors lined up to audition and when we finally came up with a cast list, a few dropped out because 'I didn't know I had to be naked on stage.' Those actors proved to be very unprofessional, and ultimately also quite ignorant. Even if you aren't familiar with the musical *Hair*, a quick Google search will show you what it is and that it requires nudity, at least in one scene. Not to mention that the audition form warned actors about nudity."

The bottom line is: do your research! This research will also guide you when selecting the monologue to prepare. As we said before, sometimes you will be informed if the director wants to see pieces from the play or if he/she has other specific guidelines. If no guidelines are given, we would recommend you choose a monologue that deals with some of the same themes as the show for which you are auditioning. Another successful approach could be to find a monologue where the character in the monologue shares some traits with the character you are auditioning for.

Last but not least: if you are auditioning for a comedy, don't prepare a dramatic monologue unless the director specifically asks for it. And vice versa: don't do a comedic piece if you are auditioning for *Murder in The Cathedral*.

Now that your monologue is prepared, let's discuss other aspects of your audition, such as clothing.

An audition is pretty much like a job interview; you want to look professional but at the same time you need to show who you are. Needless to say, clean clothes and shoes are always nice. (Don't roll your eyes: We've seen it all.) We wouldn't advise you to choose clothes specifically to serve the monologue. In other words, you should not

(photo credit: sirtravelalo/ Shutterstock.com)

181

be wearing a costume for your character. In an audition, we want to see the actor's performance, not a costumed character. At the same time, you don't want your clothes to hinder your performance, so don't wear anything that would impede your movements or that might distract the casting director. It's advisable to rehearse your monologue in your audition attire at least once.

Despite the copious amount of Green Room stories about so and so getting cast because of a very low cleavage blouse, girls: don't do that. You are better than that. Skirts are fine, as long as they are comfortable and allow you to move freely without self-consciousness. Again: rehearse in your attire. As for shoes, refrain from high heels and stilettos unless necessary and unless you can really rock them. For both men and women, character shoes are a perfect solution, otherwise, go for something comfortable that you have worn before and that doesn't attract too much attention. Do you really want the director to look at your shoes for thirty of the sixty seconds that you're in the room? Hair pulled back please: your face is one of the greatest tools you have, so don't hide it!

Actors should always carry with them their résumé and a current headshot to give to the director. The first things to highlight in your résumé are your name, measurements (height, weight, shoe size at least), and your contact information, including your cellphone and your personal email. On your résumé, you can list anything that is related to acting, including your education. List the roles you have played. You can list them in chronological order, or you can list the most prestigious credits or most relevant credits first.

It's important to mention the role, the title of the show, the production company, and the director. For example, Mrs. Erlynne, *Lady Windermere's Fan*, Buffalo City Theatre, John Donne. Don't neglect to list productions where you have played minor or ensemble roles, those are exactly as important as the lead roles.

If you have any special skills and/or specific training, please list it. Warning: "can eat a 16-inch pizza all by myself in ten minutes" is impressive, but it's not a special skill that will earn you the role. "I can play the banjo" or "I can juggle", however, are special skills that might be useful in a production.

As for specific training, that could be dance training, fight choreography, voice training, etc. If you have attended workshops, mention them, and remember to cite the instructor. Make sure your résumé fits on one page only. You should staple it to the back of your headshot, so that they'll stay together.

We could write an entire chapter about headshots . . . but we will try to summarize the most important things to remember about them. First, you need to look like the person in the picture. You have no idea how many times we have received a headshot and looked up to see a completely different person standing in front of us. You are beautiful just as you are! You want the director to remember you, and some directors are very visual.

Invest in a photo shoot, don't rely on your best friend's friend who just received a semiprofessional camera for Christmas and wants to try it. A professional photographer (preferably one who specializes in actors' headshots) will know exactly what to do to highlight your personality and your qualities and will have the technical tools to support his or her work.

As for facial hair, make up, and hair style: be smart. You want to have several headshots in your actor's portfolio that showcase what you look like in different conditions: with long hair, with short hair, with your hair up, with a beard, with mustache, etc.

Nowadays, most actors make their own websites, where they upload all their headshots and keep an up-to-date résumé and/or curriculum vitae. That's a smart way to go about it. If you do have a website, include it in the contact information on your résumé.

Finally, moving on to the audition, when you are ushered in, make sure you breathe! And smile. Then greet everyone. Remember that you want to come across as a pleasant person to work with, so be friendly and kind. Shaking hands isn't advisable unless the director or someone in the room initiates it.

Newsflash! They will expect you to be nervous, so . . . relax (as much as you can). Sometimes directors will break the ice and put forth effort to make you feel welcome. Sometimes they have been there all day and they are tired. Sometimes they are just as nervous as you are. Remember that the director wants to find the right people for his or her show as much as you want that role! There is a good chance that he/she is hoping that you are the one person he/she is looking for. We know you're not going to believe that, but it's true. Remember: you are entering the room without a job. The worst thing that can happen is that you won't get the job. So . . . perspective! You won't be any worse off than you were when you entered.

Quite likely the stage manager will give your headshot, your résumé, and any forms you filled out to the director as you enter the room. Other times, the director will already have your paperwork when you come in. After greeting everyone, state your name, the play your monologue is from, and the playwright. When you are done, thank everyone and exit. Clean and simple. Quite likely they will let you know if and when they will have call backs before you leave the room, or else the stage manager will take care of that later.

That's it! You did it! We would strongly recommend that you reward yourself. Get an ice cream, a hot chocolate, a pat on the back . . . something! What happens after the audition is out of your control, and although the waiting game is excruciating, there is no way around it. The best thing you can do is to let it go, and not think about it too much. Don't call the theatre every day to inquire, don't pester the stage manager with questions. Don't worry: if you are called back, you will know.

So far we have focused on monologue auditions, but did you know there are other types of auditions as well? Sometimes the director will have you do what is called a cold reading. With a cold reading, you will be given **sides** (short selections from the script) and, with little to no time to prepare, you will be asked to read a role. Cold read auditions can be scary, but they can also be very exciting. When doing a cold read, it's important to remember to actively listen and stay in the moment. The following exercise will give you some experience with cold reading.

Group Exercise: The Cold Read

Note for the group leader/instructor: For this exercise, you will need to provide several sides for the actors to work with. You will play the role of "director" in this exercise. You should assign specific roles to specific actors.

Step 1 – Quick Decisions
Take a minute to read over your sides and make quick decisions about your relationships and what you are fighting for.

Step 2 – Cold Read
Introduce yourself as you would in an audition. The group leader/instructor will assign you a partner to read with. Read your side, actively pursuing your goals and listening and reacting to your scene partner.

Step 3 – Discuss
What was challenging about this cold reading? In what areas were you successful? In what areas could you use improvement? Were you able to stay engaged with your scene partner, actively listening and reacting to what you were given, in the moment? Do you think that you would prefer monologue auditions to cold reads? Why or why not?

Step 4 – Repeat
Try it again. You can try a different role or employ different strategies to the same role.

Terms to Remember:

Cold Reading   Sides

Session Two

Getting the Part

It's not uncommon for actors to go to dozens upon dozens of auditions before they finally get a part, so don't be discouraged if you don't get cast in something right away. Keep trying and trying and eventually you will get that phone call, or see your name on that cast list!

Finding out that you've been cast in a production can be the most exhilarating experience for an actor. You are going to get the chance to live life through your character's eyes, feel his/her emotions and journey into a new world. If it is one of your first productions, it can be even more exciting, and perhaps a little intimidating, since you don't quite know what to expect.

In this session, we are going to talk about a typical rehearsal process, one that you are likely to encounter early on in your acting career. Remember that all productions are unique, so the process might look different in different situations (sometimes, for example, you might be expected to come to the first rehearsal with your lines memorized). This will simply give you a general idea of what you can expect. Regardless of the production, one thing is consistent: you should always bring your pencil, your script, your character journal, your creativity, your openness and your positive attitude to every rehearsal.

The first rehearsal will likely be a **read through,** sometimes called a table read. All the actors, the director, and other members of the production team will gather and do just what it sounds like: read the script. This is not a full-out performance, you are not trying to impress anyone; instead, you are simply hearing what the script says, engaging with the other characters, and really listening to them.

In the early rehearsals following the read through, some directors like to do "table work" before moving on to blocking rehearsals. This table work could include talking through motivations, tactics, obstacles, etc., discussing research related to the play, and listening to ideas that the actors bring forward. Some directors will jump right into blocking rehearsals, forgoing table work. During blocking rehearsal your will learn and/or create your blocking, work through the character's motivations, and develop strong relationships with the other characters in the scene. Remember, as we mentioned in the past, some directors are authoritarian when it comes to blocking while others develop blocking more organically, taking cues from the actors in order to build the most collaborative performance possible. If you want to be successful in your acting career, you should learn to work well with both types of directors.

You are typically expected to be "off-book", with your lines fully memorized, the second time you run any given scene, so make that your goal. Most likely you'll be allowed to call line up until tech week, at which point you should be able to do the play without that handicap. A note about calling line; when you call line, simply say "line" and wait for the stage manager or assistant stage manager to feed you the line. As soon as you remember what you are supposed to say, say it and continue on in the scene. Don't interrupt the flow by stopping to apologize, saying "thank you" or beating yourself up. Stay in character. Everyone needs a line every now and then. Just remember where you messed up and review the trouble spots on your time.

At the end of any given rehearsal, the director will usually give notes, meaning, he or she will tell the actors changes they should make, let them know things that they should repeat next time, and suggest new ideas or pose questions to encourage the actors to delve deeper into their roles. It's important to listen intently during notes. This is the time you get to glean from the director, learn his/her vision, and work together to improve the play. Even if you don't agree with a note you are given, don't argue. You can always go to the director and ask for clarification later, but while notes are being given, it is not the time to enter into a lengthy discussion. Remember that everyone wants to go home eventually and the director probably has many more notes to give. Try to just accept the note and do what the director asks. If you give it your best shot and you are still struggling to make it work for the character, go to the director and see if he/she might have some advice or a different suggestion.

Another important thing to remember is to never direct other actors. Their work is their work, your work is yours. It is inappropriate for one actor to give "suggestions" to another actor about how their scene should be played or how their character should be interpreted. It is the director's, and only the director's, job to direct.

Towards the end of the rehearsal process, you will begin running longer chunks of the play: full scenes and entire acts. Make sure you are always ready to enter on cue, and you remain focused on and offstage. A key to getting cast again is earning a reputation for being a hard-working, respectful actor. Theatre is a small world and you don't want to be known as difficult, distracted, or a diva.

Your final rehearsals will consist of tech rehearsals and dress rehearsals. This is when you will add in the all the technical elements of the production. During these final rehearsals, please remember that the members of the production team, including the director, have their hands completely full, so try and do you job with patience and grace.

The rehearsal process can be exhausting and emotionally taxing, but it is an experience like no other. From auditions all the way until opening night, enjoy every minute of the journey!

Exercise: Final Scene Showing

Step 1 – Prepare
Find a quiet place to prepare for your scene showing, using any methods you've discovered that help you feel connected to your character's emotional state in this moment of the play.

Step 2 – Apply
Perform your scene for the group or class, applying all the skills that you have developed during the last fifteen weeks.

Step 3 – Discuss
What have you learned that has helped you the most in your scene performance? What will you take away from your experience with this scene work? What moments in your scene are you most proud of? What moments in your scene did you feel the most connected? How has your work with this scene developed and improved?

Terms to Remember:
Read Through

Go Deeper

A Professional Perspective

Mark Paladini, CSA, entered the NYC casting world directing hundreds of commercial auditions for a group of innovative New York commercial casting directors in the 1980s. His shared film casting credits include New Line Cinema's *The Mask* and *Mortal Kombat*, Disney's *Spy Hard* and Richard Attenborough's *Closing the Ring*. His T.V. casting credits include *Bablyon 5 and Beverly Hills, 90210*. Mark is the U.S. Casting Director and Co-Executive Producer of indie features *If I Were You, A Previous Engagement, My First Wedding, Happily Ever After*, and *Love of My Life*. His shared television casting credits include *Beverly Hills, 90210*; *Babylon 5*; and *The New WKRP in Cincinnati*.

We had the privilege of interviewing Mark Paladini. In this session, we will look at that interview.

We asked, "what do you appreciate the most in an audition?"

MARK PALADINI: I usually appreciate an authentic personal connection to the material, which usually includes a sense of truth, emotional depth, and humor.

We asked, "what is the most common mistake that you see in auditions?"

PALADINI: Inexperienced actors usually look at their sides when the reader is talking. Experienced actors know that their intuition will work better if they take the lines from the reader rather than trying to find their next line on the script.

We asked, "what advice would you give actors in regards to selecting an audition monologue?"

PALADINI: Find a role that is appropriate for you and always make sure that you reveal just as much about yourself as you do about the character.

We asked, "do you have any advice for actors in regards to their location right out of college? Should they move to a particular city?"

PALADINI: I strongly recommend starting in a strong regional area where actors can build up their résumé. If they choose to move to New York or Los Angeles, I recommend keeping in contact with your regional agent and making yourself available for "local hire" roles there.

We asked, "do you have any advice for young actors wanting to gain visibility?"

PALADINI: "It is essential to do theatre and continue taking acting classes. Also, figure out what your bread and butter is and focus the majority of your time getting work in that direction. So many actors are so general about their goals, that they don't know how to focus their action steps towards attaining any specific goal."

We asked, "is an agent really important? If so, how should young actors go about getting one?"

PALADINI: Agents are essential to professional actors. The best thing to do is to get an agent excited about your work through doing good work. This means getting work on your own, and understanding that even though you eventually have an agent, it remains your job to find work.

We asked, "do you recommend actors participate in summer stock and/or community theatre? Why or why not?"

PALADINI: I think it's essential for actors to continue practicing their craft. Summer stock and community theatre provide opportunities to practice your craft. The more you practice your craft, the more you'll be prepared when a more high-profile opportunity presents itself.

We asked, "what are the most common mistakes you see in regards to headshots?"

PALADINI: Trying to perform in your headshot is a mistake. Also, gimmicky headshots are a mistake.

We asked, "would you rather work with a great actor who has a bad attitude, or a great person who can also act?"

PALADINI: Life is too short. Problematic actors should know that what goes up. . . . must come down. An actor should be a community builder. A friend once said, "Every show has a potato." Don't be the potato.

We asked, "what are your top etiquette 'dos and don'ts' of an audition?"

PALADINI: Don't make excuses why you didn't read the script. Don't apologize in the audition room. If you're late, apologize to the assistant and trust that it will get to everyone else. Don't criticize your acting after you've auditioned. Sometimes people love you and your self-criticism talks them out of it. Come prepared. Don't make it look like you're winging it. Avoid stylized worlds and cartoony choices – don't presuppose that the world of the play doesn't have real people in it. If you videotape your audition, upload it to a video service that allows "unlisted" links. Also, keep your other auditions as unlisted links, because you don't want someone viewing your audition to watch another audition that you've recorded. Avoid props and costumes when auditioning, but wear clothes that make you feel like the character. Avoid dialects unless they're specifically requested. Also, it's best NOT to audition with a dialect if it's required and you don't do it very well. The exception is if you do a different dialect that could appropriately replace the one requested.

Group Discussion: Mark Paladini's Advice and Conclusion

Discuss the advice given by Mark Paladini in the above interview. How do you think you will apply his advice to your acting career? What advice did you find most helpful or enlightening? Discuss what you have gained from your work with your group or class over the past fifteen weeks. What will you take away from your experience? How has your acting improved during your time together? What will the next step in your theatrical journey be? Do you have the confidence needed to move forward in the world of theatre and "conquer the stage?"

References

Adler, Stella. *The Technique of Acting*. Bantam, 1990

Bogart, Anne and Tina Landau. *The Viewpoints Book: A Practical Guide to Viewpoints and Composition*. Theatre Communications Group, 2004

Bruder, Melissa, Lee Michael Cohn, Madeleine Olnek, Nathaniel Pollack, Robert Previtio, Scott Zigler and David Mamet. *A Practical Handbook for the Actor*. Vintage, 1986

Chekov, Michael. *To the Actor*. Routledge, 2002

Cohen, Robert. *Acting One*. McGraw-Hill Education, 2007

Hagan, Uta. *Respect for Acting*. Wiley, 2008

Linklater, Kristin. *Freeing the Natural Voice: Imagery and Art in the Practice of Voice and Language*. Drama Publishers/Quite Specific Media, 2006

Lugering, Michael. *The Expressive Actor: Integrated Voice, Movement and Acting Training*. Routledge, 2012

Meisner, Sanford. *Sanford Meisner on Acting*. Vintage, 1987

Shakespeare, William. *Hamlet. Oxford World's Classics* (G. R. Hibbard, Ed.). Oxford University Press, 1987

Shakespeare, William. *Othello* (Michael Neill, Ed.). Oxford University Press, 2006

Shurtleff, Michael. *Audition*. Walker & Company, 2003

Stanislavski, Constantin. *An Actor Prepares*. Routledge, 1989

Wilde, Oscar. *Lady Windermere's Fan*. Penguin, 1940

Index

academic theatre, 158
actor. *see also* hypokrites
    character determination, 107–110
    importance of, 5
Actors' Equity Association, 158
Actors' Studio, 13
Adler, Stella, 13
antagonist, 73
arena space, 10
art, definition of, 1
assistant stage manager, 6
auditioning, 179
    etiquette, 181–183
    professional perspective, 187–188
    typical rehearsal process, 185–186

beat, definition of, 3
Bethany, 73
bigger picture, 69
Black Box, 10
Blind Walk exercise, 125–126
blocking, 11, 49, 185
    memorization game, 11–12
body, 141, 147
    creations, 36
    group exercise, 147–149
    versus voice, 151–153
    worksheet, 154
breathing practices, 49
business, 27

call line, 4
"captain of the ship". *see* director's
    view
casual plot, 69
center stage, 11
central event. *see* climax
character, 75
    applying learned skills, 101–102
    interview, group exercise, 82–83
    journal, creating of own, 97–99
    personalizing of, 91
    senses, using of, 93–96
    worksheet, 103
checking in exercise, 19–20
Chekhov, Michael, 33
Chekov, Anton, 13

choreographer, 6
classic monologue, 173
climax, 70
cold read exercise, 183
colorful nerves and dreams, 20–21
company, 23
connection reading exercise, 85
copyright, 5
costume designer, 6
costume shop manager, 6
crew, 6–7
cue, 4
C.Y.B.E.R., 143

database of experiences, 33
director, 5
    view, 155
        playground, 157–158
        respect playwright, 161
        worksheet, 162
        your playground, 159–160
downstage, 11
dramatic monologues, 174–175
dramaturg, 5–6

enunciation, 144
episodic plot, 69
exposition, 61

falling action, 70
fight choreographer, 6
final scene showing exercise, 186
found spaces, 10
French Scene Breakdown, 3
French Scene, definition of, 3

given circumstances, 75
The Glass Menagerie, 135
Greek monologue, 174

Hagen, Uta, 13
Hamlet, 70, 73
handwriting, 48
house, 11
Humana Festival of New American
    Plays, 5
hypokrites, meaning of, 1

imagination, 31
    exercise for, 37–38
    look around, 33–34
    purpose of, 49
    recreate and retell, 35–36
    worksheet, 39
improv, 27–29
incident improv exercise, 86
"informed" imagination, 98
initial event, 70
invisible scene partner exercise, 171

journaling, 97–99
    coloring the gray, 97–98
    focused freewriting, 98–99
    image collection and, 99

King Lear, 127

Lady Windermere's Fan, 169–171
lighting designer, 6
linear plot, 69
listening, 119
    shifting focus towards partners
        when on stage, importance of,
        121–123
    space, or environment, exploring of,
        127–129
    trusting your partner, importance of,
        125–126
    worksheet, 130
live performance, beauty of, 122
long speech. *see* monologues

"magic if", 115
Mandela, Nelson, 19
Marks, Laura, 73
master electrician, 6
Meisner, Sanford, 121
memorization, 47–50
memory, 41
    experimentation of, 49–50
    memorization, 47–50
    recreating physical environment,
        51–52
    senses, awakening of, 43–45
    shuffle, 47–48
    worksheet, 53

The Method, elements of, 13
Method Acting. *see* Stanislavski
      Technique
modern acting, father of, 13–14
monologues, 163
    for an audition, 173–175
    analysis of, 169–171
    definition of, 165–167
    team, 166–167
    worksheet, 176–177
Moscow Art Theatre, 13
music director, 6

nervous energy, 20
new world fairytale exercise exercise,
      87–88

object check-in exercise, 93–94
"off book", meaning of, 3
open air theatre, 10–11
open scenes, 55
    choosing of, 57
    developing of, 61
    eight open scenes, 63–66
    personalization of, 101
    with secret, 134
    switching of, 59
    worksheet, 63

Paladini, Mark, 187–188
    advice and conclusion, 188
paraphrase and morph exercise, 123
people watching, 14
period play, 75
Pipino, Kiara, 122–123
planet customs exercise, 24–25
playwright, 5
    importance of, 161
plot, 69
producer, 5
professional actors, 159
proper breathing, 143
properties master, 6
proscenium theater, 9
protagonist, 73
Punchdrunk, 10

raising the stakes, 115
    exercise, 116
read through, 185
reading, memorization technique, 48
recreate and retell, 35–36
Redmayne, Eddie, 159
rehearsal
    etiquettes for, 159–160
    process, 185–186
rehearsing, memorization technique,
      48–49
relaxation, 145
research, script and characters, 75–76
resolution event, 70

reversal event, 70
rising action, 70
Romanov, Anastasia, 35–36
Romeo and Juliet, 133
room recreation and scenarios, 51–52

scenes
    scents in, 95–96
    score, 109
        evaluation of your, 109–110
        list of actions in, addition of, 113
    showing of, 102, 138
scenic designer, 6
script, 3
    analysis, 70–71
    and characters, 67
        people who are involved, 73–74
        research, 75–76
        what's happening?, 69–71
        worksheet, 77
    in hand, meaning of, 3–4
    and scenes, 79
        first reading of scene, 85–86
        journey, 81–83
        worksheet, 89–90
        world of the play, 87–88
secrets, 131, 133–134
    surprises, 131, 135–136
    unexpected gifts, 137–138
    worksheet, 139
senses, awakening of, 43
    group exercise, 43–45
    using of, 93–96
sensory memory, 13, 43
Shakespearian English, 75
sides, 183
Sleep No More, 10
small group script work, 5
The Society of Art and Literature, 13
soliloquy, 166
song lyric improve, 29
sound designer, 6
stage directions, 3
stage fright, defeating of, 19–21
stage left, 11
stage manager, 6
stage positions, 9–12
stage right, 11
stakes, raising the, 115–116
Stanislavski, Constantin, 13–14
Stanislavski Technique, 13
step on stage, 17
    improv, 27–29
    lean on me, 23–25
    stage fright, defeating of, 19–21
    worksheet, 30
story, 69
Strasberg, Lee, 13
strategy switch-up exercise, 112
substitution improv, 94–95
subtext reading exercise, 85

supporting characters, 73
surprises, 131, 135–136
    creation of, 135
    group exercise, 136
survive and win, 105
    changing strategies or tactics,
          111–113
    character determination, 107–108
        facts of, 108–110
    raising the stakes, 115–116
    worksheet, 117
suspension of disbelief, 24

table read. *see* read through
tactic phone call exercise, 111–112
take the space in and react exercise,
      128–129
team story, 137–138
teammate qualities, 23
technical director, 6
theatre
    fundamentals
        as art form, 1–2
        modern acting, father of, 13–14
        need for, 2
        stage positions, 9–12
        unique about, 1
        vocabulary, 3–5
        worksheet, 15
    games, group discussion on,
          23–24
    spaces, group discussion on, 11
    who's who in, 5–7
Thespis, 1
thrust configuration, 9–10
timeline, 159
tongue twisters exercise, 144–145
trust fall exercise, 125

underscored imagination
    part one, 33–34
    part two, 34
upstage, 11

Vakhtangov, Eugene, 115
vocabulary, 3–5
vocal relaxation, 145–146
voice, 141
    versus body, 151–153
    connect your breath, 143
        part one, 143–146
        part two, 146
    group exercise, 143–146
    worksheet, 154

"want" reading exercise, 86
Williams, Tennessee, 3, 135
word association popcorn, 28–29
world of the play, 75
    exercise, 87–88
writing, memorization technique, 48

CPSIA information can be obtained
at www.ICGtesting.com
Printed in the USA
LVHW01s2340201217
560213LV00006B/11/P